Clouds of Heaven, Beings of Light

Clouds of Heaven, Beings of Light

Sharon Kay Casey

Winchester, UK
Washington, USA

First published by Circle Books, 2015
Circle Books is an imprint of John Hunt Publishing Ltd., Laurel House, Station Approach,
Alresford, Hants, SO24 9JH, UK
office1@jhpbooks.net
www.johnhuntpublishing.com
www.circle-books.com

For distributor details and how to order please visit the 'Ordering' section on our website.

Text copyright: Sharon Kay Casey 2014

ISBN: 978 1 78535 169 3
Library of Congress Control Number: 2015939709

A CIP catalogue record for this book is available from the British Library.

Design: Stuart Davies

Printed and bound by CPI Group (UK) Ltd, Croydon, CR0 4YY, UK

We operate a distinctive and ethical publishing philosophy in all
areas of our business, from our global network of authors to
production and worldwide distribution.

CONTENTS

Introduction   1

The Answer   3
The Call   4
The Laundromat   6
The Voice in the Closet   10
Protection Lost   12
The Paint   15
The Landlord   16
Digging in the Trash   19
There is Hope   22
The Voice   25
A New Start   29
Tossed to the Four Winds   30
Separated from God   33
Reunited   34
The Intervention   36
Be Still and Know   38
The Door   40
Home   41
The Celebration   42
Beings of Light   46
The Water   49
The Altar of God   53
Sharing the Story   57
The Lord Works in Mysterious Ways   59
The Book   63
Instructions for Life   65
Reaching the Broken   67
What Scars are for   70
The Scars   72

The Temple of Living Stones   77
The Continued Path   85
The Voice for God   88
Curtain Call   92
Shared Thoughts   99

Resources   112

A special thanks to my neighborhood friends, who lived on Emerson Avenue, Modesto, CA, in 1969.

Special Thanks:
This story would not be complete without the help and support
I received from my family and friends.
In grateful gratitude, I send a heartfelt thank you to those who
supported me beyond measure.
And those are:
Judy Almand, Mark Pingleton, Daniel F Griffin, Calico Hickey,
and Hector Hernandez for his permission to add his part to this
story. My mentor and friend Paul Tuthill, and last but not least,
Scott Osborne, thank you Scott for listening.
Know that wherever you go, my love goes with you for we are
one and the same.
I love you, I thank you, I appreciate you, and above all things, I
see the spirit of Christ the Light of the world in you.
Thank you for being here now!
Light and Love,
Sharon Casey

Introduction

There is nothing special about me. We are all equal in the eyes of our Father. We are all equally loved beyond measure, equally given all that we need, equally filled with that which is of Him: light, life, and unconditional love that is forever eternal. This love has no beginning and it has no end. It simply goes on and on and on, that which we are cannot and will never die. There are no exceptions. "That which is of God will never die and there is nothing that is not of God."

How does one describe the indescribable?

With trust the words will come to paint an ever so faint memory of that which lives and dwells in us all.

I ask, "How do I describe that which has been described so many times in so many beautiful and truth filled ways? There is nothing left to say, I am not even a writer." And I hear Your voice, "Write it down, it does not matter how many times it has been described. Do not concern yourself with how to describe your experience it will come. Remember the truth in one is shared by all, remember that. There is nothing that can be said that has not already been said, there is nothing that can be shown that has not already been shown. There is no other who can describe home like you. There is no other whose witness can be anything more beautiful, profound and unique as the one you are to share with the World, my one love, my one creation. Be a voice in the seeming darkness of forgetfulness; remind them who they are."

The truth in one is shared by all: the memory of Home dwells in all as surely as it dwells in one.

Where to begin? Would I share this experience when my eyes opened? Would I start when I called Scott Osborne (DJ at KYCC in Stockton California), to not only thank him for listening to

1

God, but to thank him for acting on what he had heard and felt? Or would it be as I drove down the road that beautiful morning and asked with a sincere heart and open mind, "Was it a dream, it seemed so real?"

Some twenty years ago, I had a dream or at least I thought it was a dream. When I woke up or should I say closed my eyes, it was all I could think of, flashes of this dream would flood my mind... until the day I asked if it were real: "Was I there, it seemed so real, or was it a beautiful dream?" I thank you, Father for answering me in such a way that it cannot be denied.

The Answer

As I was driving, early one morning, on my way to Petaluma California, I had continuous flashes of what I thought was a beautiful dream. I pulled over and asked the simple yet profound question, "Father was it a dream, or was I there?" I knew the answer would come, I knew not how, yet I had faith. I looked about me and said aloud, "radio" the answer will come through the radio. I put the question out of my mind and went about the day. As I was driving home late that afternoon, down 580 eastbound near Livermore. I was tuning the radio, searching for some music. What I heard was a man's voice announcing; "Remember that dream you had the other night? Stay tuned I have the answer you are waiting for." I heard the call letters of the radio station and that it was a Family Christian radio station.

When he returned there were angelic voices singing in the background like a mass choir of soulful angels. He repeated what he'd first said, "Remember that dream you had the other night... and you wondered if it was real or a dream? Well I am here to tell you it was real... you were there; you were in Heaven with God. And God wants you to know you are still there." He went on to describe it in more detail. I do not recall anything that was said at that point. I was ecstatic. It was as if I were floating off the seat. I was laughing, with tears flowing, thanking God for answering me.

"I thought you would pick the radio to answer me and you did. Thank you, Father." I do not recall making my way over the Altamont that day. I do recall pulling over and sitting there for the longest time. Remembering my experience of home, remembering when I opened my eyes, the light bodies, and the movement, the river, my Lord, and all of you.

The Call

It took me a couple of days to find the radio station once again. Finally, Scott, the DJ, announced the call letters. I stopped at the nearest gas station that had a phone booth. I called information and they gave me the phone number of the radio station.

I called the station and Scott Osborn answered. I had no forethought of what I would say, I only knew it was important that I call him.

I said, "Hi, my name is Sharon Casey and you do not know me. I called because I wanted to thank you for listening to God."

Scott was of course bewildered. I went on to state, "Remember a few days ago when you came on the radio and said, "Remember that dream you had? It was real, you where there."

He replied, "Yes I do remember that."

I asked him, "Why did you say it?"

He said, "I am not sure, it just came to me."

I then said, "That morning I prayed and asked God about a dream I had. I was wondering if it were real or a dream. God answered my prayer through you, Scott. And I just wanted to thank you for listening to Him. Through you, Scott, God is answering prayers."

He was exuberant and so excited. "What do you mean?" he asked.

I said, "I was in Heaven."

He asked if I could hold on and I said, "Yes."

When he came back, I went on to tell him briefly about what I saw.

I told him, "Heaven is a place of bright light, yet it does not hurt our eyes because we see through the eyes of our spirit." I went on to explain that we are golden cloud-like beings of light, with human form and beautiful. I told him Jesus was the first one I saw and that there was a celebration. We were being danced "in" and that I was spun around so fast it made me feel dizzy, even though I did not have a body. I was not aware of that at first. I said there was not one thing in Heaven that is earth-like or of this world. I told him that God was there and that we looked like Him. He was huge and full of lights that flashed and spun around and that some of them were different colors and He had beams of light that flashed from the top of His body, from His head.

Scott was amazed, he was laughing and praising God, and so was I. Together we marveled at the wonders of God, how He truly works in mysterious ways. I do not recall every word that we spoke that day. Yet I can promise that Scott did not doubt, and neither did I. We were equally humbled and filled with awe, praise and heaven's joy.

Blessed are those who have not seen and yet have believed. John 20:29

I felt as though I was floating after Scott hung up. I felt the greatest joy. I was beaming at everyone there at that gas station, as I found my way back to my truck. I climbed into the cab and sat there staring off into the dark blue sky with my experience rolling through my mind. The color of the sky took me back to the late 1980s to the day I was at the laundromat.

The Laundromat

It was just another day; everything that could go wrong went wrong. I was used to it. I was stuck in a relationship I could not get out of. I refer to it as the Seven Years of Hell; it was nearly five, yet it seemed like thirty. I was stuck in a world of intravenous drug use, blackmail, and abuse. It was a cycle I'd started back in my early twenties, full of abusive boyfriends and meth. At the time, I thought it was ok to take it a few times a month more of a recreational usage. However, that attracted the broken guys, who had different agendas, which was to get high as often as possible. The boyfriends changed, the scenery changed, yet the outcome and the circumstances stayed the same. All except this one relationship. It was my breaking point, and looking back from where I am now, I'm grateful for it, yet at the time it seemed to be the worst thing that could have happened to me. I longed for release daily, yet there seemed to be no end in sight.

Until one afternoon, standing in the middle of the local Laundromat, a stranger changed my life. Here's the story, simple and brief, yet none the less profound.

It was just one of those average days. I was out of money, out of luck and feeling I would never escape the muck I had sunk into. My washer had broken down, which was nothing new. So, rather than watch the mountain of dirty clothes pile up, I decided to gather them and go to the Laundromat. When I arrived, I was just a bit surprised to discover I had the place to myself. Was my luck beginning to change?

As the clothes were washing, I set mulling over my life as it was. I recall feeling insignificant and much less than ideal. I felt stuck in a life I did not want, with no escape.

A car pulled up outside. The driver got out and started looking in the back seat of his car. He put his hands on his head, walked to the back of the car, and started digging around in the trunk. He was a Middle Eastern gentleman who immediately extended a hello as he walked through the door. He was mumbling something to himself.

He was tall and a bit on the slender side, maybe late twenties. He had this glow about him; for lack of better words, he was "shiny." I felt not the slightest bit threatened by his presence.

He carried with him a handful of clothes, and I mean a handful. No doubt what he had dug around in the trunk for. I remember thinking, *"Why did he even make the trip? He had nothing to wash!"* I got up to check on the washing hoping that, if I stood there and stared long enough that it would somehow speed up the process.

As I stood doing the "washer stare", this gentleman called out the name, "John."

Now this stopped me in my tracks. I looked around there was just the two of us there!

I asked him, "What did you call me?"

He paced back and forth a few times and replied in a stern voice, "You heard me."

By now he had my full attention. He stopped pacing, looked me in the eye, his eyes beaming with a warm gentle smile and said, with a slight accent, "I was sent with a message for you." Right then and there that cold void I would refer to as my heart, felt as if it was becoming engulfed with the warmth of love, a feeling that rushed over me so that tears began to swell.

These are the words he gave me, "Why so weary? Your journey is almost through. Be glad."

I turned looking out the plate glass window into the blue sky, with tears now streaming. For a moment, I saw myself as a little girl three years old maybe four. I had awoken with a sense of urgency. I ran to my parents' room. I can still see myself standing by their bed in the middle of the night. "Wake up Mommy!"

My mom opened her eyes with a startled sound in her voice, "What honey, what?"

I said, in my little three-year-old voice: "Will you write for me?"

She of course told me to go back to bed. I was persistent and she, being the loving mother that she is, got up. I am sure she thought if she were to get any sleep at all, the only way to quiet me down was to pacify me. And that she did! I can still see her sitting there, in the chair by the lamp, with a notepad and pencil. And me standing there singing this little song. To me it was important. The words were something about the sky and clouds. I do not recall any of the words or the tune. What I do recall is my mama showing me what she had written down. Although I could not read, I trusted she did what I had asked. As I sit here writing this, I realize my three-year-old self was reaching out to me. My three-year-old self had reached out from my innocence to tell me that I am love. I had reached out through the seeming passage of time to save myself from all I had thought I had done wrong.

Still looking out the window I replied to my messenger, "I know... I know."

At that moment my answer was not referring to the laundry, and neither was his message. And I knew that! I stood there for a moment or two, then turned, still wiping the tears from my face and said, "Yep, my clothes are just about finished." I had to play it off.

He hesitated for a moment, and then smiled at me very attentively. He knew!

As I gathered up my clothes and headed out the door, he just stood there all smiling and shiny. Feeling much lighter than when I went in, and a bit bewildered, he called me, "John?" How often I have wondered if he knew that those simple words he spoke to me I would hold forever dear. Of course, at the time I had no idea how dearly I would hold them.

Even now, when I think myself small, and insignificant, in times when it seems the world has turned its back on me, and I wonder what the hell I'm doing here. Whenever I feel cold, and in need of warmth; when I forget who it is we are... I open that small box of treasures I cradle deep within my heart. Thus echoes the words I've heard so many times. Knowing what I know now, that no man is an island. And that nothing is truly received unless it is given away. I would extend to you these simple words I hold so dear. That you too may draw them in, and find encouragement in their simple meaning!

Why so weary?
Your Journey is almost through, Be Glad!

The Voice in the Closet

To reach my children I would recreate the hell that they made, and I would walk through it with them, so they can see my love for them. And I will pull them out of their shadowed places, and clothe them in Light and fill them to overflowing with my eternal love and living water.

Creator of All Things

I took the laundry home and started putting it away. I opened the closet door and put the clothes on hangers. The closet was small and dark and as I stood looking in, I felt goosebumps flow over me in waves. It was a very calm feeling. I then heard a voice say, "Give me your life."

It was a male voice, deep and soothing. I said, "What?" out loud, and He repeated, "Give me your life."

"My life?" I said aloud. I felt myself quiver. Still standing in the closet, my eyes closed and my head bowed, I had a thought of what it would be like; I envisioned myself being a missionary in some Third World country, putting my life in danger and not having any toilet paper. Funny how my mind thought back then! I walked over to the bed and sat by the nightstand; I could hear Him talking to me, saying everything would be ok. I could feel His love, and my heart began to ache deep within my chest and I cried in a whisper, "Lord, I'm not ready yet, let me suffer a bit longer, for the world, and for what the world has done to me." I heard His voice. It was the sound of the deepest agony... I heard Him groan.

Looking back from where I stand now, this was the door opener. This was planting the seed. He knew I was not ready to accept that I had created all this. And that the world had done nothing. That all suffering would be gone, if I could accept that I was God's Child and that He loved me beyond measure. Instead,

I saw myself a victim and those who lived in the world with me were all victims as well. The world was suffering as deeply as I suffered; I just wasn't ready to give all that up.

My sheep hear my voice, and I know them, and they follow me. John 10:27

Our Father always allows us to have what it is we truly want. I had asked to suffer. Although I was suffering, apparently there was so much more from where that came from. I had asked for more. This is not something God gives us; rather it is what we give ourselves. I prayed often for my family, that they are kept safe from harm. Yet I did not ask of anything for myself, I knew what He wanted and I was not ready.

When you hear my voice, harden not your heart. Jesus

Protection Lost

At the time, I had a boyfriend living with me. He had been with me a little over two years. I would refer to this time as the seven years of torturous hell. Even though it was but five years, it seemed more like thirty. The day I opened the door and let Satan in would be a deep regret of mine for many years to come. I had invited him in and then he would not go away. For the sake of this story, I will not call him Satan, I will call him something a bit nicer... how about Goober? Little Goober face, yes, yes that will do (smiling)!

I'll share a few tidbits with you from the time I let Goober in the door, up to the time of the missing paint and the landlord.

The first month was not all entirely bad. We were playing house and getting high, seemed he liked doing it much more than I did, yet at the time I overlooked that, until one early morning when he asked if I'd take a walk with him, which I did. We went down the street about a block and ended up at someone's house. He told me to wait outside, which I did. Then a bunch of people came out of the house and someone else pulled up in a car.

Goober walked over to me holding a check, and said, "Do you think you can cash this?" It was someone's personal check written out to no one and had the amount of sixty dollars.

I said, "No," and argued over the fact that I did not know who it belonged to. To my surprise, this statement got me a hard punch right to the center of my stomach. I bent over gasping for air; it hurt so much. He yelling at me and a few of the guys standing in the yard were laughing. I knew I would not get any help from them. Eventually I gave in, just to get away from that place. I was confused, sad, and scared. I did not know any of these people and had no idea what any of them were capable of.

While walking towards the store, where I would try to cash this check, I was hoping they would refuse it. Of course, I was trying to get out of it! This got my hair pulled and my throat choked. I had realized later that I had lost my Mother Mary gold pennant and chain. I had worn this necklace for many years without taking it off. To me, at the time, it was my protection and it kept me safe. Now it was gone!

The store cashed the check and Goober took the money and gave it to the folks that were at that house. I hoped I never had to see them again. Eventually, the store informed me that the check came back, and of course I paid it. I was so happy I did not get in trouble for it.

Within a short time after this incident, I asked Goober to leave and of course it was a fight. I told him, "Fine, then I'll leave." I gathered up some clothes and my kids, and while I was heading for the door, he walked up and kicked me with his Army boot right to my shin. I fell on the floor. The pain was unbearable. Since I could not walk, I could not leave. Through the years, I would often look down at the large dent in my shin and rub it, feeling the indent the size of a boot toe and feeling hopeless. During the first year, there would be several attempts such as this and they always ended up in an ugly way. I would suffer through many a lesson such as this one.

There were threats of blackmail. The one that held me captive was the one of setting me up, putting me in prison, and having my children taken from me. I had called his bluff on a few occasions. It was proven to me that he would follow through with his threats.

Looking back from where I am now, I would say to myself, "Child, I love you, please forgive me for not allowing you to feel that love. Your innocence and trust was never harmed; you were never what you thought you were. You have always been perfect and loved beyond measure, as you are a child of God and extension of Love itself. Do not be afraid of the love you have within you. As it is who you truly are. It is who you have always been and nothing can or will ever take that from you."

Concerning the life journey of those who have found their way out of the deepest darkness, back into the light of love, this is a life oftentimes of deep suffering and loss. We gave ourselves all this just so we could know the true meaning of love by forgiveness. It cannot be any other way. Be happy that you chose such a life and be joyous that, that which we lived is not who we are, but what brought us home to God.

The Paint

Not long after the time of me hearing God's voice, my landlord had stopped by to drop off some paint. I had been painting some of his rentals for him. He had come by very early in the morning. I got up to answer the door and I asked him to leave the cans on the front porch. There were about six gallons. I went back to bed and heard someone knocking on the door again. I got up and opened the door to find a car full of people in the driveway. Then some guy I'd never seen before said Goober owed him money and he wanted it.

I said, "I do not have any money."

He said, "I'll take the paint then and we'll call it even."

I could have tried to stop him, yet he seemed a bit scary to me. I was just glad he took the paint and left.

I called the landlord to tell him the paint had been stolen and he was pissed off. He had every right to be upset, yet I didn't realize just how upset he was. When the rent was due that month, I went to cash my check at a local grocery store. I walked out of the store and there was my landlord waiting for me. He had never done that before. I handed him the rent money expecting a receipt.

Instead he said, "This is for the paint, where is my rent?"

I tried to explain to him that I did not have money for the paint. Looking back, he may have thought I did it on purpose because he had not paid me for the work I had done. I did not mention that it was because I was trying to prevent a fight or something worse. Of course, I could not tell him that and I soon forgot all about it, hoping it would pass.

The Landlord

As I have mentioned, when we ask to suffer, God does not stand in the way. He will not give it to us Himself, yet He will allow us to give it to ourselves. We create our own shadows and then we live in them believing that they are real.

About a month had passed from the time the rent was paid, and it was time to pay rent yet again. It was payday. I was off getting dope. I had left the rent with Goober to give to the landlord. When I came home and asked if the landlord came by, I was told, "Yes." I asked for the receipt. Goober said, "The landlord didn't give me one." That seemed a bit odd to me. I said something about it, yet really did not think much of it. Towards the end of that month, late in the afternoon, in rushed an officer showing a badge, stating we had fifteen minutes to get out. I was in the bedroom folding clothes and went into the kitchen to ask, "Why?" He showed me the papers. He was extremely agitated and authoritative. I was in shock; I had no idea. I had figured out later that we were served notices. Goober had not given them to me. To this day, I have no idea why he would have done that. It meant he would not have a place to live either. I know it could have been resolved if I had only known.

I started packing clothes. I was told I could not by the officer. So, I grabbed my purse and walked out. I was numb all over. My girls were off swimming at a friend's house, so all they had were their swimsuits on. It was late July. We had no place to go. So, we just stood out front of the house. After the officer left, I went into the house to get clothes, toothbrushes, etc. I turned around and there stood the officer.

I was arrested for trespassing. As I was driven off to jail, there on the front porch were my dogs and my Persian kitty Gismo. Goober took the dogs to his mother's, but I never saw Gismo again. I spent many a day and night walking the neighborhood calling for him. To this day, it breaks my heart. I had bought him from my landlord who raised Persian cats. I am sure someone, maybe even my landlord, took him in and cared for him. I loved him so much!

I spent a few days in jail and was released on time served. My girls were at a friend's house to which I cannot say the words, "Thank you" enough. My life was a blur then. Looking back it remains a blur. My first few nights as a homeless person were spent on a neighbor's outdoor couch with Goober. For whatever reason, it took me that time to get my thoughts straight.

We did not have any money. His mom took us to a hotel the third night. I felt that Goober and his mom were waiting to see if I would come up with somewhere to go. I couldn't, I was just too numb. The hotel she took us to did not allow pets. Goober had two little dogs.

His mom said, "You are going to have to take them to the pound."

Goober became furious and starting yelling at me. I replied, "Why are you yelling at me? I did not say anything, your mom did."

In response, I received a hard kick with those Army boots of his, right between my legs. He kicked me so hard I fell to the floor screaming in horrific pain. As I lay crying on the floor, his mom took the dogs and left. I do not recall much after that. What I do recall, however, is that I could hardly walk without pain. I was swollen and bruised for some time after that.

There would be many more hotel stays. We stayed with a dear friend of mine for a few weeks. By that time, I had gotten my thoughts together and was able to retain a house to rent. I was on a program for low income housing which was a blessing. And even though I had lost our house, the program still allowed me to stay enrolled. I only had to pay a few hundred dollars to the landlord that kicked us out. Although it seemed like a very long time, we were without housing for just a little over six weeks.

For me to go through the daily struggles, the fighting and the drug use, would be making stuff up because I recall very little of it. I can say life was hard, yet not always; we had fleeting moments of happiness and laughter. My children were a mess most of the time, only because I was not there for them. Both of them stayed with friends off and on. Looking back, I am grateful they both had somewhere to go where they were cared for and had someone there for them.

Digging in the Trash

Goober and I spent much of our time trying to get money. The one sure way was aluminum cans.

We would get up early just as the sun was about to rise, and off we'd go walking the alleyways looking in every trash can. We knew what day the garbage trucks ran. We would go out just ahead of them. Goober always held the bag while I did the digging, which should be no surprise to anyone. We spent at least one or two days a week digging around in other folks' garbage. There were a few who would put dog poop and things like cactus on top. I can't say as to whether it was done as a deterrent or just the way things ended up. None the less, it never seemed to stop me from getting the aluminum cans out of their trash.

Not far from where we lived was a grocery store that had a large red plastic container out front where folks could put their cans. The container was approximately ten feet tall with an opening just to one side towards the top. It was within reach to allow disposal of cans. I had this great idea. We should go down at night to get the cans out. So, we began keeping watch to see when it was picked up by the recycling place. We planned on getting as many cans as possible the night before it was picked up. So, on the night before pickup we gathered as many trash bags as we thought we could carry and went down to the bin. Of course, I went into the bin, with Goober's help. The bin was so full that I was up to my waist in cans. Have you ever tried filling trash bags in the middle of the night with cans? It is impossible not to make a bunch of noise. I filled the first bag and had difficulty getting it through the hole. So, I started tossing the cans, one by one, out through the opening. Goober would pick them up off the ground and toss them in the bag. It was comical to say the least.

Goober would say, "Be quiet a car is coming." So, I would sit and wait until he said the coast was clear. After we filled the bags, I found I was not able to get out of the bin. I tried several times and just didn't have the strength to pull myself up. I finally came up with the idea of piling as many cans as I could just under the opening where I was to get out. I was able to get myself lifted up just enough to get out. We walked home with our trash bags full of cans and me minus one shoe (it fell off as I was climbing out).

The next morning, we took the cans down to the recycler and got a bunch of money. On our way home, we stopped by a park to rest. I was so tired. I recall sitting there lovingly adoring a tree we were sitting under. Goober said, "Let's go get some cigarettes," and started walking across the park. I got up and went straight towards the tree, wrapped my arms around it and pushed my face gently and lovingly into its trunk. We were giving each other what we both needed, comfort and support. The tree felt so alone and so did I. Goober turned and laughed at me. "Come on," he said.

Me, still standing with my arms around the tree said, "No I want to stay here." I looked at Goober, standing there with a sparkle in his eyes, his baseball cap, scraggly hair and a big smile on his face. There was a glow about him. Something I had not seen before; this would be the image of him I would carry with me through the years.

This image of him would be the one in which I found forgiveness. It was this moment that would set my brother and myself free.

The deepest darkness is a place we created. Filled it with tar and dove in. Then, wallowed in it until it was all we knew. We tarred and feathered ourselves hoping no one noticed. We slithered in and out of alleyways and avoided street lights, as we may have been seen for what we thought we were. Covered in dark goo with the feathers of angels we had killed while they were trying to remind us of who we were: Children of God hiding within their own shadows. We were hiding in shadows, which we made up, in our own imaginations and thought them real!

There is Hope

There would be a few short stays in different houses until we ended up at my grandfather's house. My grandfather was the one person in the entire world who loved me no matter what I did. He saw something good in me and showed me true uncondi-tional love. For this, I am forever grateful.

We intended to stay with my grandfather only temporarily, until I could finish truck driving school and get back on my feet. Through a series of events, the meth available in the area had dried up. All that was available out there was not any good, in other words it was bogus.

So, Goober and I had stopped taking it. Yes, surprising as it seems we actually were clean for a while. There was occasional coke use on weekends. It was the one drug where you can work all week and spend all the money on the weekend. Although life had changed for the better, Goober was still hateful, always threatening some kind of harm whenever he didn't get his way. I had gone from completely giving up to thinking there was some hope. My one thought was to get working. Somehow, although I did not know what it would be, I knew my days stuck with Goober were coming to a close.

I would pacify myself with thoughts of escaping Goober. I had all sorts of fantasies. One of my favorites was taping him up while he was sleeping and dropping him off in an orchard somewhere. By the time he got free, I would have had the time to pick up and go somewhere where he wouldn't be able to find me. Silly really, but thoughts like that would keep me going through the torturous years that I was stuck with him.

Goober had gotten his truck driver's license about six months prior to me getting mine. His first job was driving silage for a local company. Silage is what they feed livestock, mostly dairy cows; it can be corn or alfalfa. He was the one who actually talked me into getting my Class A driver's license, with the promise I would have a job driving silage when I had completed the training and had my license. I got my license and sure enough, I got the job, my first driving job. And of course, Goober was right there. I didn't mind that much.

I spent the day driving around in circles in a field full of corn. It was hard work with long hours but I enjoyed it. I had time to myself and I thought often of the day I heard God's voice. I wondered what my life would be like if I had done what He had asked of me and had given Him my life. I began praying and opened up just a bit to Him, I began thanking Him for all he had done in my life. I could see His love and protection was there all along with me and my children. I was so grateful for that. There were lots of early morning sunrises and late evening sunsets, blue skies, clouds, and a little wildlife everywhere. Being in that truck for twelve to fourteen hours a day away from Goober, I had begun to find peace, my mind was clearing. I could feel God for the first time in so many years; I could feel His love for me.

The silage job was seasonal. It ran from mid-March through late November. I was a bit sad when it ended. Yet I had driving experience now and had promised that I would find another job. And that I did. It was perfect for me. I would drive up to Tracy, about twenty miles from where I lived, and pick up cat food then deliver it to a silo nearby where it would be bagged and sold. I averaged about six to eight hours per day and that was six to eight hours a day completely away from Goober.

He had not stopped with the spitting on my face or the threats of putting my in jail. I must admit, if not for him, I don't believe I would have ever known the feeling of hate. Until he came into my life, I had been the victim many times. Yet I didn't have that deep feeling of hating anyone. I had allowed this one guy to take me deep into fear. Like a roller coaster ride that seemed to have no end, there was only spite and hate. Towards the end, I had completely given up on everyone and everything. Until I realized at last, that he could not harm me.

One afternoon in the early spring of 1991, he got mad and threatened to set me up and have me put in prison. I had heard that one, one too many times. Instead of cowering as I so often did, I looked at him straight in the eyes and said, "Go ahead, I'd rather be in prison than be with you." His eyes got real big and I could tell he knew I meant it. I think at that moment he realized he simply could not bully me anymore.

Both the Spirit and the bride say, "Come!" Anyone who hears should say, "Come!" And the one who is thirsty should come. Whoever desires should take the living water as a gift. Revelations 22:17

Call on me in the day of trouble; I will deliver you, and you will honor me. Psalm 50:15

The Voice

Late one evening I took off to the store. I found myself driving around… just driving, thinking; wondering about my life. I had this little glimmer of hope now. Could my life really change? As I drove, I prayed. I opened up and could feel God's presence. A few times, I pulled over as I could not see through the tears I was crying. They were beautiful holy healing tears. I was overcome with the release of pain, of all the pain I had allowed myself to endure and carried with me. It was so heavy I could not bear the weight any longer. I was tired, so very tired of suffering. I had suffered enough, and I was ready to give it up. I had made such a mess of everything. Everyone around me suffered as well. Because of all my countless wrong choices and because I chose to suffer; it was time; I was ready.

I did not want to go back home. I had driven around for hours. I knew, eventually, I had to go back. As I headed in the direction of home, I turned the radio on and this song by Michael W. Smith, started playing. It was, "Place in This World." I was just around the corner from the house and I pulled over again, listening to the words, wondering, "Was there a place for me?" I began to wonder what I could do? I know nothing. My life was so out of touch for so many years, it was as if the world had passed me by. I know nothing of the normal world, the average world.

And I remembered what Jesus said: "You are not of the world." John 15:19

Michael W. Smith is a Christian artist and "Place in this World" was a crossover song, one that played on secular radio and religious radio. At the present moment that song was for me. God was calling me. He was calling me not to be in the world, but calling me out of it.

I pulled slowly into the driveway, expecting to see lights on with Goober's head poking through the curtains. The lights were off and there was no movement in the curtains. He had gone to bed.

As I sat in the car in the driveway, I said aloud, "I know nothing; everything I have done on my own has led me to pain, and I have made so many mistakes. Everything I have tried to escape it has failed." I went over in my mind the many ways I tried to get away from the life I had made. It was like flashes on fast forward, going through my mind. I was crying so hard I could barely lift my head off the steering wheel. Then You spoke to me.

"I heard your voice", You said, "God... you know... God."

Thoughts went through my mind of a time I was happy. I was in church, and I was taking Holy Communion. I was talking with Jesus and angels. I was in the mountains and there were animals everywhere, the sky was blue and there were clouds. And I said aloud, "I know God, I know You." I was crying so hard and my heart felt like it was breaking in a million pieces. There was heaviness on my chest that felt like a ton of bricks.

It was as if all things had become suspended. Time had stopped. I was present with God; He was comforting me. I said, "I cannot do this. I have tried and I cannot, but You can, I know You can. You are the only one who can. It has always been You. I have tried to do it alone, take my life please... take it. I do not want it anymore, it is Yours. My life has always been Yours." The heaviness I had in my chest hurt, I could hardly breathe the pain was so intense.

I cried out, "Lord this hurts... it hurts!"

And You said, "Trust me."

I raised my head up. I leaned on the back of the car seat and looked out the side window and said, "Oh... trust."

I paused for a moment and said, "I want to, Lord, but I do not know how."

I heard Your voice... You said, "That is enough."

I felt myself fall back in the seat. My head rose skyward and the heavy weight I carried was lifted off my chest; the pain was gone. Something in me, something I had created of myself was taken, and at that moment, I was made new. I sat there a few minutes; the tears were drying on my face. There was a glow illuminating from me. Everything was brighter.

I asked You, "What do I do now?"

You said, "Go in the house it is OK, everything will be different in the morning."

I will never forsake you, any more than God will, but I must wait as long as you choose to forsake yourself. Because I wait in love and not in impatience, you will surely ask me truly. I will come in response to a single unequivocal call. Watch carefully and see what it is you are really asking for. Be very honest with yourself about this, for we must hide nothing from each other. If you will really try to do this, you have taken the first step toward preparing your mind for the Holy One to enter. We will prepare for this together, for once He has come you will be ready to help me make other minds ready for Him... A Course in Miracles
T-4, 7:8

I woke up in the morning to the phone ringing, I got up to answer it, and it was my mom. We talked for a few minutes. Goober of course was standing right there by me. And I said to my mom, "Can you come out and help me get rid of Goober?"

She said, "Honey, is he there?"

I said, "Yes." She asked me to hand him the phone. He sat down in a kitchen chair and listened to whatever my mom was saying. Within a few minutes, he handed me the phone.

My mom told to me he was leaving and asked me to call her once he had gone. I hung up the phone and expected some sort of retaliation. I expected to be yelled at, have my hair pulled or spit on, but none of that happened. Less than a half-hour had passed since my mom had spoken with him. Goober was in the car with all his belongings, backing out of the driveway. It was my car but it was OK, he could have it. It has been nearly twenty-three years since that morning, and I have not seen him since. Goober was gone and the life I had created apart from God went with him.

A New Start

By the next day, I had another car, one that was not falling apart. By the end of that week, I had another job and a friend of mine offered me a temporary place to stay. It was just for a few months until I could save money to get my own place. I had no concerns for the future. I knew God was guiding me. And I trusted that everything was going to be alright, and it was and still is exactly as it should be.

For everything there is a reason, all part of a plan to bring us home. That plan is to awaken us to who we are, the Holy children of God, in whom their Father is well pleased.

I had a strong desire to return to church; I wanted to pick up where I left off when I was but nine years old. I wanted to return to my Church to complete my studies and to become a confirmed Catholic. And that is exactly what I did. Looking back, I realize it was all part of my healing process. I was abruptly pulled from the Church when my parents divorced, not long after my First Communion. What I recall about that precious little girl is that she wanted to be a nun because she loved Jesus so much. Although she did not understand what all that entailed, she knew it meant to give her life to God.

Tossed to the Four Winds

We had a very loving home. There was no fighting between my parents that I can recall. My dad worked as an accountant for a local construction company. My mom was a homemaker. She raised poodles and also sold costume jewelry for extra cash. Back in the sixties, that was the thing to do. Both poodles and custom jewelry were very popular.

If there where issues, I was not aware of any of them. My younger sister and I lived a happy, healthy life. My sister was five and half years younger than me and I love her so much. She is my baby sister and I would do anything for her then and now.

My parents had gone through a series of hardships within a short period of time. My dad's nephew, Bob, had passed away in an auto accident. Oddly enough, we had driven by the accident scene, not recognizing it was Bob's car we were seeing. I recall my mom having me lay down in the back seat of the car. That was our normal routine stance when driving by accidents.

My dad and I took Bob's death hard. He was a good man, young and newly married. He was expecting his first child. I can recall how he would come by just to play with me, and I adored him.

Within a few months after Bob's death, my Grandpa Casey passed suddenly from a heart attack. We lived just across the street from him. My Dad was devastated of course. During these hardships, my mother was pregnant and close to delivery. It must have been hard on her as well, but she never showed it, at least not to me.

It was a few months after Grandpa's death that my little brother Richard was born. It was in November and I was in second grade at school. My dad was so excited at Richard's arrival that he came to my school and announced it to me and all my classmates who were within earshot.

I was so excited and happy that we had another baby! I had a little brother to go along with my little sister. I was the big sister and I liked that feeling. I ran home from school that day. We lived only a half block away from my school. I was staying with our nextdoor neighbor who was watching me while my mother was in the hospital. No sooner had I come through the door when the phone rang. The neighbor, whose name was Georgia, hung up the phone with a sad look on her face. I remember her calling me over towards her.

She looked at me in the eyes and said, "Honey, that was your daddy, your little brother died."

That was the bomb that blew my family up. Some years later my Dad would say, "Satan came in and tossed us to the four winds."

It was the beginning of the end for my loving family and home. My mother started sleep walking all the time. There were a few times she was put into jail. The police thought she was drunk. My dad still worked, yet missed many days. He would often lock himself up in his study to write. He expressed his self that way. I think it helped him work through the sadness.

Of course, financial problems began to pile up. Dad went on a few spending sprees. For example, he bought a brand new red Plymouth Barracuda. We took a bunch of nice long drives after that. It was a really pretty red car. Then Christmas rolled around, my little sister and I got all kinds of really nice gifts. One of mine was an organ with two rows of keys. It had a bench made of pine. I played it every day.

By the time spring had rolled around, there was noticeable strife between my parents. It revolved around my dad's excessive spending and Mom's sleep walking. Picture if you will my dad, trying to keep Mom in the house at night, and my mom trying to get my dad to control his spending. Neither one was getting through to the other.

On the day of my First Communion it had become obvious to

me something was horribly wrong. My parents were not happy with one another. The next day my dad left our house saying he would be back. Shortly after, some people came and took the car, and some other people came and took my organ. My grandparents came and took my little sister Suzy.

It had been six days since my First Communion. It was a Saturday, the day of my second confession. My mom and I got into our car with a few things I needed. I was going to join my little sister at our grandparents' house. At least, we would be together. My mother was explaining to me what had happened. I had several questions, yet my biggest question was, "We're still going to go to church though, right Mama?"

Her answer was confusing and I did not understand it. I recall being so upset and deeply angry. She said, "Neither your dad or I can be Catholic anymore."

I asked, "Why?"

She said, "Because we are divorcing honey and the church excommunicated us. We cannot go to the church ever again."

I asked, "How am I going to get to church?"

She said, "I do not know."

Separated from God

And as I was being driven out of town, on that last and final day, my mother drove me by the church. I wanted to take confession one more time. I recall the church seemed so big and it was empty. I stood there after blessing myself, taking it all in. It was just me and God and the silence. As I looked around, all I could think was that I did not want to leave. I wanted stay. I remembered one of the nuns had told me that God was everywhere, and that He lived in me too. I recall thinking about that but I did not really understand it. To me, I was leaving my Jesus, my best friend.

I made my way up to the altar, my shoes clicking on the shiny floor. I felt a warm comfort and peace. I felt God's love for me. I bowed before the altar and slowly walked over to the confessional. I went in and tried to close the door slowly, but it slammed shut making a loud noise. I do not recall every word exchanged between my younger self and the priest. What I do recall was making up things I had not done wrong. After all, I was there to confess, I had to say I had done something wrong; I must have sinned although I could not think of anything. So, I just made stuff up so I could stay, stay there with God.

I went and said three Hail Mary's and one Our Father, just as the priest advised me. As I walked out of the church, I felt empty. I felt empty because I had left myself sitting in the confessional. That precious child of God, she did not want to leave. And I knew she would be safe there. I just had no idea at the time how long it would be before I would retrieve her. I had no idea so many years would pass. Nor that she would remain where I left her sitting in the confessional making things up that she had done wrong. The little girl that walked into that church that day was not the same little girl who walked out. It was still me, just not all of me. It was an angry me that felt empty.

Reunited

Not long after my return to church and my Confirmation, I went back to Saint Mary's. I entered through the side door. It still looked the same, only not as big as I recalled. I blessed myself and lit a candle. I recall the late afternoon sun was streaming through the stained glass and lighting one side of the pews in a soft golden haze. I walked to the altar and bowed, and then I walked over to where the light was shining and sat down. As I closed my eyes to pray, I heard a door slam just behind me. I turned to see who it was but no one was there. The sound seemed to come from the direction of the confessional door. I turned around and closed my eyes, and I heard it slam even louder than before, except this time I also heard what sounded like footsteps running, they were short and quick and made little clicking sounds on the floor. It sounded like they ran into the pews just a few rows back from where I was sitting. I turned around, and for some reason I was not surprised to find no one was there. I could not see her but I could feel her. I smiled, and turned back around; my visitor ran up another row of pews and waited… and then ran into the row right behind me. For a moment in my mind, I saw "her" standing there and she ran into my arms. I could feel her love. In God's presence, we were at peace. My younger self and my older self were reunited; joined back together in a beautiful moment of complete healing.

As I sit here, writing and reading this story, taking it all in, I realize I experienced in this life that I chose, the same thing that we have all experienced and believe is true. I experienced being separated from God. And it punched a hole in me; it broke my little heart into eight billion pieces. I experienced the emptiness we all feel. I tried to fill it up with that which is outside of myself but I could not. The hole became like that of a magnet to the darkness, except the darkness was not that which came from outside of me, but from me.

The healing power of forgiveness born of love will reach across all seeming boundaries of time to heal God's children... Nothing is impossible.

In truth, we are all sitting in the confessional, the confessional of our minds. We cannot think of anything we have done wrong. Because we have done nothing wrong; neither to our true selves nor to our Father. To our Father we are exactly the way we were created, perfect, and wholly loving. Being our Father's children that we are, when we make things up they become very real to us. And we think ourselves lost, we are lost in all things we made up and have made real. When we step out of ourselves for a moment and take a long look, it is amazing. Our creativity goes so far beyond comprehension.

The Intervention

Sometime had passed since my new life had begun and my life could not have been better. I was working for a local trucking company that hauled feed commodities to mills. I had a nice big house where everyone was happy and living a life that we had never had before, yet it was as though it had always been that way.

Have you ever experienced time in slow motion? This is where all that is in you and about you slows to nearly complete stillness. I have and it is unmistakable. Late one afternoon, I took a load of feed to a local milling company just as I had done one hundred plus times. It was my last load of the day and I was tired and ready to go home.

A simple explanation of my job would be: the feed is poured into the top of the trailers at one mill and taken to another. The feed is then delivered by opening the bottom of the trailer and it pours or falls out into what is called an auger. An auger closely resembles a large screw that turns and moves the feed into an elevator that delivers it to a silo or container of some sort. This particular afternoon I had finished unloading the feed and was sweeping up around the pit. The pit is the opening in which the feed is poured. At the bottom of the pit is the auger. I had taken the grill off the pit as the opening was small; it was about four and one-half feet long and two feet wide and maybe three feet deep. As I was sweeping, I forgot I took the grill off and stepped into the open pit.

Immediately everything within me slowed to a near standstill, it was as though I could hear the stillness. Someone was whispering to me, keeping me very calm. I was being talked through it. My left foot went to the side of the moving auger. I moved my foot very slowly with the auger (screw), to where I was finally able to lift it out. Just before it would have been too late and the end of my life would have been the result. That should have been what happened and to anyone else it would have, but it did not happen to me.

I fell to the ground and rolled away from the pit crying out, "Thank you, thank you... Thank you for saving me." I heard what sounded like a crowd sigh with relief. I was not alone.

It was amazing, I had scratches on my chin, forehead, both knees and my elbows had large deep scrapes; both knees on my pants were torn. I had what I later affectionately referred to as my "watermelon bruise:" ...my entire left thigh was black. It was as though I had been chewed up and spit out, yet I lived.

For he will command his angels concerning you to guard you in all your ways; they will lift you up in their hands, so that you will not strike your foot against a stone. Psalm 91:11

Be Still and Know

Within a few short days after the accident at the mill, I had an amazing experience; it was the ultimate experience that one can have while in the body. Up to now, this has been a story. I have given you a brief overview of the life I had chosen before I had this experience. And preceding, I will give you a brief overview of the life afterwards. It is not my life that matters, it truly is neither here nor there. It is a story, a simple story, one many can relate to, yet all in all it is a story, it is my story. What matters is the heart of this story, the purpose of it, not the beginning nor the end but the heart. Within the heart lies our memory of home. And so without further ado...

My love, it is now my great privilege that you and I go there together... For it is together we all go the way to God... take my hand!

With your permission, I would ask that you would step out of this story with me for just a moment. Gather with me now. Yes, I know it is a bit dim here and we can vaguely see one another in this place that is before the dawn, but look, just there, you see that light? That light is our home; no, we do not need to travel there. I know it seems so far away, simply focus on it, and it will come, for we are already there.

I have much more to say to you, more than you can now bear. But when He, the Spirit of truth, comes, he will guide you into all the truth. He will not speak on his own; he will speak only what he hears, and he will tell you what is yet to come. He will glorify me because it is from me that He will receive what He will make known to you. All that belongs to the Father is mine. That is why I said the Spirit will receive from me what He will make known to you. John 16

When stillness comes flowing over like a well springing from the depths of our being... We see your face, faint at first then brilliantly shining with many lights brighter than the Sun itself. We witness the universe moving within you, swirling slowly, then like a spiraling vortex with lights of many colors, like precious stones of unspeakable brilliance. Within your being, surely all the heavens dwell. Beams of lightning extend from your head and we your Children of Light stand in awe and wonder.

The Door

I laid down one night long ago. I found myself running through the deepest darkness towards a flicker of blue light. I felt calm. I was simply present; there was no fear. As I ran, the light would move and I would lose sight of it. I would spin around until I found it, and again, I would run towards the light. This continued on, until I realized the light was not moving; I was zig-zagging. I was zig-zagging in the deepest darkness, searching for light that was right in front me. Once I realized this, I stopped. I found the light once again, which was growing now in both size and brightness; it was no longer blue and flickering. It was now a whitish yellow. This time, I did not take my sight off the light. I ran towards it until the light was all I could see. I then entered the place of Light that was inside me, within my mind. I stood facing what looked like a solid wall or gate. It was pure white and shimmered like a pearl. To my left there was a large doorway opening. It was sky-like inside this opening, very faint light blue with something similar to small formed misty white clouds moving about. They were all moving towards the opening of the door as if they were peering in, watching... me.

I then heard the voice of a female behind me speaking to someone, she said, "She's ready." Then out from behind me came what looked like a young woman dressed in white. She had dark brown hair and eyes, her skin was light in color, and she was beautiful. To me, she was an angel. She stood in front of the wall or gate and looked me up and down. She nodded her head in agreement. I then stepped through the door.

Home

As I attempt to express what I saw, what I felt and heard while my eyes were open, I feel it is important that you know there is nothing of the world we see around us that is in our home. Yet, in my attempt to describe our home, I will use words of what we think, see, and know of in this world. Like gold, precious stones and water. Be assured that nothing of this temporary world exists in the place that always has been and always will be.

Concerning colors, our home is very gold in color. Consider every shade of the spectrum of gold with yellows and white multiplied one million times, then add the illuminations of a brilliant crystal. These are the colors of our home.

Concerning the unification of family members and friends, I promise you they will be there to meet you when that time comes and you leave the body you think you have now, when you awaken from the dream. Yet my experience and calling is to share with you, so that you can remember who you are.

Truly all the heavens will be rolled up like a scroll and the earth will be no more.
Revelations 6-14

The Celebration

My first recollection after I entered the door was that I was surrounded by a bright golden mist that was everywhere. As I focused, I noticed something that was moving just in front of me. This movement began to have form, the form was of a golden cloud-like figure. And I was being moved around. It was like we were dancing, swirling, twirling around with this golden figure, who, to me, had a familiar and very beautiful light. As I was being moved about, I noticed there were other golden cloud-like figures everywhere. I attempted to focus on them. However, I was then lifted up high by my golden-figured partner in a huge swirling, spinning motion, I was spun around so fast that I felt dizzy, yet exhilarated. My eyes were blurry, or so it seemed, but I continued to attempt to focus on the figure before me.

There were many golden cloud-like figures higher as well; they gathered around me. It was as if they were taking turns. I felt they were each saying something. I could not hear what they were saying, but I could feel them, I could feel their love for me. They were of all sizes and shapes yet golden and cloud-like, each of them unique and beautiful. I was then placed by this brilliant being of light to the side of where we were dancing. As I stood in awe, I witnessed another golden figure danced in by the same one who had danced with me. I felt a joy within me that was beyond exuberant. I was not sure of where I was, I knew nothing. I was like a small child looking at the world around me for the very first time. I had no memory of the life I think I have now. I knew that what I was seeing was a celebration.

The celebration was taking place in an area that was brilliant white. It was sparkling like diamonds. It ran as far as I could see from my left and my right. It seemed to be like a solid wide walkway, the golden figure of light was standing and dancing on it. I stood right at its edge. This is my place prepared for me before time begun!

My vision was slowly beginning to sharpen, and I found myself gazing down into this white way. What I saw was movement of something not solid at all. There were trillions of what looked like diamonds. They looked and moved like small comets, layers upon layers of them, it was like they were swimming, they were swimming around. This was a river I was looking at, like nothing I have ever seen. I wondered, *Where am I, what is this place?*

My eyes moved from one edge of the river across to the other side. On the other side of the river, I saw hundreds of golden cloud-like figures. I noticed that they too were looking about. I thought, *Is this Heaven?* I then heard a female voice behind me, she said, "It is okay."

I went to turn to see who was talking and was asked not to. "Do not look behind you," she said.

I asked, "Why?"

I then heard another female voice speak saying something to the one who had answered me; she then said, "All you want to see is before you."

I had now turned from facing the river. I was looking forward to the front of this golden place... somehow I knew it was the front, yet I cannot say how I knew. There were many golden cloud-like figures standing in front of me as well; they too were facing forward. As I looked at the back of one of the figures that was there standing right in front of me, I began to notice a form, just beneath the outer golden mist. That was when I knew that the golden cloud-like forms were spirits. Their form was like an outline of a human body. Seeing this prompted me to look at myself, as my head was moving downwards to see what my body looked like.

I heard one of my guides behind me say, "She is going to look at herself." I heard a sound of concern in her voice. No doubt, the concern was for my reaction. They did not seem to know what to expect from me.

What I saw was amazing. I was golden, with an outlined human form. I could see pearlized white lines running through my lower body like veins, but not veins. I looked at my arms and they looked the same. I peered down to the place I was standing. It was a shimmering golden mist, yet clear like glass. I was a child, filled with such awe and a peace I cannot describe. I looked around and lifted my head to see what was above me; the sky was white yet clear with golden alto cumulus-like clouds that were in layers and appeared to be moving. An illuminating hue encompassed everything. What caught my attention was a place between the whitish mist and golden clouds. I noticed a very faint light blue, a patch of blue. I recall looking at it and wondering. It was familiar to me, yet I could not quite place it. In that moment, I did not recall what it reminded me of. (It reminded me of the earth sky.) I had forgotten this place, this place where I think I am, where I sit right now sharing this with you. I had forgotten this world. I had forgotten it as if it were a fleeting dream I had in the night.

I lowered my eyes. To my left, towards the upper level of spirit bodies, I noticed that towards the front there were some spirits that were faint, very mist-like and golden-yellow in color. They were very large, huge even. I cannot say how many but there were several of them. Although I was not told this, I knew these huge spirits were never human. They never experienced the thought of being separate from God. They were angels. They are the Archangels. They seemed to be conversing with one another. And one that I was looking at in particular was looking at me too. There was a communication, yet I do not recall what it was.

There was some movement going on at the front. There were golden spirit bodies making what looked like a mound. They were lying on top of one another, and it appeared, they were merging as if they were building something. I then looked back to my right, towards the river to witness the Celebratory dance of many. The one that was with me had now taken on not only a human outlined form, but it seemed he was wearing clothes. He had an outline of clothing and the one with whom he was dancing had an outline of clothing as well; she looked to be from another era, maybe the early 1800s. The dance for her was gentle and slow like a beautiful waltz.

For whatever reason, seeing this is what prompted me.

I then shouted out, "Where am I?" before my guides and angels could stop me.

All of heaven stopped for a moment. Then the dancing continued, although I was told nothing. I then knew I was home; this was heaven. I heard my guides sigh behind me, as if they were relieved.

Oh how the water sparkled as I witnessed the multitude of golden light bodies in celebration. Some in a slow dance and some spun and swirled about, with feeling of unceasing joy; indescribable peaceful bliss.

Behold, I tell you a mystery; we shall not all sleep, but we shall all be changed, in a moment, in the twinkling of an eye, at the last trumpet; for the trumpet will sound, and the dead will be raised imperishable, and we shall be changed. 1 Corinthians 15:51-52

The veil is torn, step through to the light.

Beings of Light

You will see me coming in the clouds of Heaven. Revelation 1.7

We, His children, are the clouds of golden light, filled and overflowing with living water.

I would like to take this opportunity to describe our bodies; describe what I saw.

As I have mentioned, each spirit body I saw was unique; some were brilliantly defined. Some faint yet beautiful. Those I saw that were faint were more of a misty yellowish shimmer and transparent with a cloud-like form.

There were many who were various shades of light to medium gold. Their density was thick and they were of a cloud-like form. There were a few who were golden, yet with a human body outline. I could see their arms, legs, and heads, even their center body. I even recognized a faint image of facial features. Within them, I could see what looked like veins, pearlized in color. Some had many veins and some had but a few, those who had few were filled with a golden shimmer and their bodies were not as pronounced.

Most spirit bodies had a design of light reflecting through water. Then there were but a few, maybe five, that were golden, possessing a full human body outline with what seemed like clothing. This was for me, to see how they would appear in human form. I cannot be sure of the reasons why I was privileged to this vision.

There was one trait that all had. Within the center of their being, approximately where our human umbilical cords would be, there was a circular place of brilliant lights that moved about like the stars in the heavens. The lights were swirling in a clockwise motion. If you were to take your hand, stretch it out and place it over your belly button, then that is about the size of this circular place of many moving lights. The lights resembled stars. Most of them were white, yet some yellow, blue, red every color one can image. I found myself looking attentively at this area in everyone who was facing me, from the other side of the river.

What love we have for one another, Agape love. The love we feel, the love that is all-present, is beyond the simple words we use to describe the feeling. It is simply indescribable. All that we believe ourselves to be in this temporary world is nothing but a dream except for those who know they are not a body and have a glimpse, perhaps a thought or an idea of who they are. Know the truth… all that we seem to be is nothing in comparison to our true selves.

Concerning our size, each spirit body has a similarity with the human body. We are tall, short, petite; some are slender, some not so slender. When it comes to making a comparison with our size, we could be as large as the universe and as small as a pinhead. Yet it does not matter because we are home.

As I stood looking about, I noticed I did not hear anything. There was dancing yet no music. There was silence in Heaven, a still silence. The silence carried with it a knowing, a knowing of thought; thought that is shared by all. Nothing is hidden as there is nothing to hide.

I felt completely comfortable and relaxed. There was no physical feeling at all, no pain, anxiety, feelings of stress. I was simply present while any feeling that would stem from fear was not. Neither in any other nor me. I somehow knew that. I looked down at my chest area, I was breathing. I took one conscious deep breath. We breathe in Heaven; Our Father the Creator of all things is the air we breathe.

We all stood in amazement. I noticed others looking about, and there was so much to see. Although I had no sense of time, there was order. We all stood in the place we were given, ushered, if you will, by Jesus who is the Beautiful Light Being that celebrates our wakening with a celebratory dance of joy, the Wedding dance.

For those who may feel dismay at this statement, please do not. Our Father knows nothing of religion, and cares not of what path you took to awaken. It matters not! I cannot speak for who will celebrate your awakening; yet, I can promise it will be all of us. I can share that which I experienced, what I saw. That is all I am asked to do. All that God created is good, and there is nothing that God did not create.

When it is complete, all will be awakened. All will know they are in Heaven our true Home. That which is the beginning, from where we came, will be the end. It is the place to which we shall return. The Beginning and the End, this is God's will and nothing will ever change that, it simply is what it is.

Everyone is unique and everyone is the same, in our home we are individuals with the same thoughts and all thoughts are true, as there is nothing one can think that all do not know, my thought is your thought and your thought is my thought. In this place, we join together and create ONE body of Light. This is what we have always been.

Your journey is almost through. Be Glad.

In my Father's house there are many mansions: if it were not so, I would have told you. I go to prepare a place for you. John 14.2

The Water

I stood along the river's edge, with adoration for the one celebrating our awakening. As I have mentioned, He is a beautiful golden spirit, yet no different than any of the spirit bodies that are here in this place.

Dear friends, we are children of God, and what we will be has not yet been made known. But we know that when he appears we shall be like him, for we shall see him as he is. 1 John 3.2

Jesus' outward appearance is tall, His hair long, slightly longer than shoulder length, yet groomed and pulled to the back from the sides. If I was to describe His body, I would say He is of average build, He had a slight tummy and broad shoulders.

I cannot say how many I witnessed waking or how long the dance continued. I witnessed Jesus standing on the river, the dance was complete, yet the celebration had just begun. I witnessed Him moving towards the edge, on the side of the river where I was standing. My eyes were fixed on him. He was moving towards me. "His face... He was looking at me." I imagine I glowed ever so brightly; there was a vibration within me which can be described as a purring cat lying on our chest. Although He was a golden spirit, I somehow knew His hair was dark; He had a beard that went from just below his ears to the chin along the jaw and a mustache that outlined his mouth, both were well trimmed. His brows were bold and his eyes may have been brown when He was in human form, yet being His true self standing before me confirmed that His eyes were the color of fire.

He stood in front of me on the river and I faced him, I am wholly present with Him in this instant. He is beautiful; my love for Him has no description. He smiled at me.

And said, "Welcome!" (Until this point, I had heard nothing other than a few words my guides had whispered to me). He looked at me, moving His head as if to look me over.

He then took my right arm and held it out and said in an almost surprising voice, "Why, you are…"

I looked at Him and said, "What, I am what?"

He then looked into my eyes and said, "I have to do this."

I could see His lips moving, he was saying something, yet I could not hear what He was saying.

I said, "Wait, I can't hear You."

As I watched His mouth move, I felt a great calm. I stopped trying to hear, as I could feel what He was saying; I slowly moved my eyes up his face and looked deep into His eyes. It was as if I was drawn into His eyes, I soared within Him. I moved past what reminded me of speeding by a picket fence. What I was doing was looking to the side. I turned my head and looked forward and saw stars, except they were not in darkened skies, they were in light, beautiful light. I soared like a shooting star through His spirit, a star that burned brighter instead of fading out. I soared to my place within the spirit of Christ.

It was as if I were a child about to be born, I was floating, or so it seemed, my knees were tucked up and my head was down. I felt a sudden gush within the center of my being. It was as if the floodgates of a huge overflowing dam had been opened. And the water was flowing within me; there are no words to describe it. As I went to stand, I could hear singing, it was everywhere, it was the air itself. Like an unseen Angelic choir. Singing praise with a sound so beautiful, like nothing I have ever heard before or since.

When we are home, our movement is effortless and fast, there are no constraints of time, gravity or physical bodies… nothing is impossible. There can be a one-on-one communication with everyone at the same time. It is like being in a thousand places at once. That would be impossible for this temporary world and these temporary bodies, but not in our home where we are our true selves. This communication is without words or sound.

With the sounds of heaven, of home enveloping me to the highest Joy, I looked to see my Lord was not standing there by me. I wondered where He went. My guides reassured me, "It is Ok, He is welcoming others... see?" I turned my head downstream to my right and saw Him standing before another. There are so many, we are all here now. All have awakened from what seemed like a very long sleep.

I found myself looking down into the river, so beautiful; diamond-like comets swirling and moving about, truly it is a river of life.

I stepped out onto the river with my right foot and it felt solid, I then looked towards the front to the mouth of the river from the place it flowed, from its source. And there I saw two spirit bodies standing on the river as well. They were both on the right side of the river of life. One was tall and slender and the other of average height and build. Both appeared to be wearing clothing, both were golden and had a full body appearance. They were looking toward me, and then they both turned and looked toward the front. I could see the tall figure holding his hands together in front of him, as one would in prayer. The other spirit held his arms out wide and his head titled up, he was praising God.

I shouted, "How Long", my voice sounded like loud thunder to my spiritual ears, and it was as if I had gone into a trance of a sort for but an instant. The air around me was like a rainbow, like light streaming through a clear crystal. I watched the air reverberate with the sound of my voice. I did not know what my face looked like. I can only imagine my spiritual mouth was wide open as the wonder of all this was nothing I had ever felt. Our home is truly beyond description.

The time is now... truly nothing is as it seems... that which was seen through eyes of fear and dread has come to pass and we have found it was Love all along. And it would be in Love that it would present itself to its Children...

The time is now.

There will be no more delay, but in the days when the seventh angel is to blow his trumpet, the mystery of God will be fulfilled.
Revelation 10 1-11

Be Glad.

The Altar of God

*Jesus said, "If they say to you: Whence have you come? say to them,
We have come from the light, the place where the light came into
being of itself. It [established itself], and it revealed itself in their
image. If they say to you, Who are you? say, We are his sons, and
we are the elect of the living Father. If they ask you, What is the sign
of your Father in you? say to them, It is movement and rest."*
Gospel of Thomas 50

I stepped back to my place, and looked to the front to the golden
misty mound of spirit bodies that was now growing wider and
higher. I saw a spirit body that was running from where we were
standing, towards the mound, he stopped and looked behind
him towards those of us who were gathered. This spirit was
golden, full-body with an appearance of wearing clothes; it
looked like he was wearing a button-up short-sleeved shirt and
pants. His face was oval; he had a large frame and average
height. Once again, I seemed to know his hair was black, his eyes
brown, in his human form he was ethnically Hispanic. He was
looking in my direction and waving his arms. I lifted my arm,
and waved, and he waved backed. I had no idea who he was, yet
he seemed to know me and wanted my attention. He was facing
us, with the mound of converged spirit bodies behind him and I
watched him, he had a look of amazement, it was as if he was
giving one last look. He then turned and ran towards the
converged spirit mound and dove right into the center of it. I
could see him as his spirit body conformed and became one with
the others. I wondered what they were doing, not in a concerned
way, more in wondrous, amazing presence, observing, with a
childlike wonder and a feeling that one cannot describe. We are
building the altar of God.

As my vision continued that night, I saw someone like a son of man coming with the clouds of heaven. He approached the Ancient One and was led into his presence. Daniel 7:13

I stood in awe, and at that moment I watched a streak of light that moved like fire in a windstorm, it moved down the river towards the mound. This was Jesus; He merged into the converged spirit bodies and was now standing on top of them, which had taken on an appearance of solid golden light; it was flat on top like a platform. Jesus stood atop to what was my right, as I stood facing the front. He became brighter, more brilliant than the sun; He grew in size to three times that which He was at the beginning, within him were millions of lights that were growing as well, becoming the size of stars in the night sky. I saw to the left flashes of what looked like the outline of a brilliant rainbow, it was arched and shimmering. I could see a very faint illuminating figure, beginning to appear beneath the arch, it was 100 times the size of any other spirit bodies.

To the center, between Jesus and the large spirit body, I saw a faint misty yellow spirit begin to appear, it was brilliant and illuminating, its size was that of Jesus, three times that of any other spirit body. As it formed, it moved towards the front of the altar and stood in the center. The large figure became more brilliant; within I saw lights beginning to move, vibrant colors spinning, slowly at first then they became larger and moved like a swirling vortex. This being was God! This being is our Father appearing to us in a form. The yellow spirit in the center is the Holy Spirit born of the Father and of the Son.

As I watched, the Father grew more vibrant in form and size. I looked over to see that Jesus was still present yet very faint, as was the Holy Spirit. Towards the top of the Father, I began to see many bright white orbs spinning, it was as if they were moving in and out from a deep place within Him.

I would like to mention and you may know by my description

and your own inner knowledge, that God our Father is truly neither man nor woman, and neither are we. True, some of us have the appearance of male or female like that which we thought we were in our human forms; however, that is a temporary image that we are projecting. There is a feel of masculine and feminine. Yet we are all on the same level, there is no specialness here, there are none that are smarter or richer. Put very simply, "We Are" in the most ultimate sense of the word. And our love for one another is the love of all loves, that which we seek so desperately for in this life that we think we have is that which we have now and forever in the place we never left, that is our home.

All are amazed; we His children are witnessing the event we have awaited, and that is to stand as our true selves before our Father completely awake and present before Him. We witnessed our Father grow to the size of the altar. The spirit of Jesus and that of the Holy Spirit had merged with His spirit. Now there is what looks like galaxies spinning within Him. His skin is like a rainbow with an illuminating shimmer of the whitest white. His form is that of a great arch. I saw a beam of light brighter than lightning emerge from the top of Him into the spirit bodies just to my left. The spirit in which this light was sent was present, yet looked as if a flame consumed it; the spirit was less pronounced now than the rest of us. I saw another beam emerge like lightning, it went just to the right of me, to the other side of the river towards the front of the spirit bodies.

I had a thought: Tell my children about God, I accepted this thought even though I did not know who they were or where they were. I looked towards the Father and saw a very bright white light, my one thought was, "No." The white lightning-like beam that extended from our Father this time was for me.

(This is the most difficult for me to write about, I did not want to come back. I did not want to close my eyes and return to this world of illusions, but He sent me, He sent me back. I under-

stand now when it was said that, "Jesus came willingly.")
Returning to this world of dreams, with the knowledge of who
we are and where we are is a joyous event. I laugh now, yet in
that moment, that seeming instant. I simply forgot to laugh.

I felt myself spinning and I could no longer see, I asked to talk
with Jesus and I heard him say I would awaken again and He
gave me a number. I was taken to an earth-like place; it was dim,
like dusk just after the sunset. I could see others there. Although
I could not make them out, as they were at a distance, I could see
their outlines.

They were being consoled, by one or two angels. The setting
was like a forest with trees and lots of big rocks with a river
flowing gently. My guides where with me still and they were
comforting me, I recall being so dismayed, I kept repeating, "He
said I could come back, He said I could come back." I don't recall
much of that, I woke myself up whimpering, and I sat up in bed
still crying, I was so sad. It was three something in the morning,
and I was back. I got up and went to the kitchen; I was in a haze
with flashes of my dream playing over in my mind, it was all I
could think of.

The number I was given was nine, the time I was given has
since come and gone. In 2002, while driving home from work, on
a windy bend known as highway 132, (San Joaquin National
Wildlife Area), something happened; I can't say what. Yet I recall
thinking, what now? And I heard your voice, I had a choice and
this time I chose to stay, to stay and write, Heaven, I'm going to
stay, and write, "Heaven the book." The voice corrected me and
said, "The movie." I in turn said, "Book" and chuckled.

In a sense, the entirety of all of our lives is like a movie. With
each of us playing the Hero role of our own story.

Sharing the Story

Right after the confirmation that my experience was indeed true and that it was not a dream, my one desire was to share it. I shared it with a few close friends, my children, and my mother. There were a few occasions when I stood out in front of the church I attended, Saint Jude's, sharing with a small yet interested crowd. I imagine that those passing by must have wondered what type of story I was sharing. I stood in the middle of my fellow parishioners, smiling from ear to ear, with a glow that I am sure must have been unmistakable, with my arms out attempting to describe the experience in a quick yet detailed manner. Answering all the many questions of what I saw.

I was once asked, "Sharon do you find that people do not believe you when you tell them this story?"

My reply, "Yes, and it doesn't matter whether they believe me or not. I am not here to convince anyone. The experience speaks for itself; the receiver is free to do with it what they will. It is real to me, not only did it happen but it is happening now. Not one moment has slipped by in heaven since my return to time, to this place of the grand illusion, where God's children, think themselves lost and abandoned, living in a world where shadowed thoughts of fear are real. How they long for escape and seek it by running even faster into the darkness they created. Not understanding that what they seek is what they are now and always have been, the Holy Children of God, the Creator of all things."

My love, why are you seeking high and low? As you are already here!

The one reiterated comment I heard was to write it down. A good friend of mine's mother was adamant about it, almost scornful, she was a Catholic prayer warrior and very charismatic in her practice.

She prophetically professed to me one morning, "Sharon you are going to write, and people all over the world are going to love what you have to say."

And of course I argued with her, "What, I cannot write, I cannot even spell. I have to use a dictionary."

Yet she insisted saying, "Mark my words, I do not know what you will write, but it will be spiritual and touch many. I can see it."

Nothing is impossible for God, anything, and everything can be.

Trust.

The Lord Works in Mysterious Ways

I have heard it said that the Lord works in mysterious ways. I was ablaze with spirit as I went about my days. I was a new creation. And I had an experience that I longed to share. Not only the story of Heaven but what God had done for me. I found myself most days sitting in my truck reading the Bible and listening to Christian music on the radio. I was still a truck driver and spent long periods of time waiting, waiting to get the trailers filled with animal feed or waiting to unload that same feed at some mill.

Most days, all of us feed haulers would start out at 4:00 in the morning at a local mill. We would all line up on both sides of a very long driveway waiting our turn to get our trailers filled. Which was most often soy meal or corn, and then off we would go to deliver our loads. And of course the earlier we got our first load, the more we could do through our twelve-hour days. And the more money we would make. So, everyone wanted to be first. There was often bickering between the drivers as to who was next. One driver was very confrontational. Several times, I witnessed him pushing another driver or getting up in their face and yelling at them. I found myself watching this man's actions with no real thought or feelings. I was observing what seemed like a very angry man. I do not recall this man's name but for the sake of this story, I will call him Jose.

And then there was Mulchor. He seemed out of place as a truck driver yet made the most of it. He was young and smiled more than most drivers. He would often pop his head into my driver's side window and ask me, "What are you doing?"

I would nonchalantly state, "Reading the Bible."

Or he would ask me, "What is that you are listening to on the radio?"

And I would reply, "That is alternative Christian music." We had several conversations about God and he was interested in my point of view. And of course I shared my stories with him on how God changed my life in an instant. He would often say something during our conversations that led me to feel he was much deeper and more spiritual in belief than he appeared to be. He often had deep words of wisdom, which I appreciated.

And then there was Pete, he owned his own truck where most of us worked for a trucking company, Pete was a sub-hauler for the company I worked for. Pete was a very kind man. He had some sort of disability, he was small in stature and very slender and he walked with a limp. He had a wife and several children. On the side of Pete's truck in bold letters stated, "Pete & Sons." Sometimes on Saturdays, he would bring them all to work with him. I would pull up and there would be his whole family in his truck cab. They looked to be enjoying themselves, laughing and talking as if it were any normal family outing. He would get his children out of the truck and show them how to tie down the trailers or have them help untie the trailers and prepare to have the trailers filled. I would watch him; he would have a little pep in his step and a smile. I loved to see him smile.

One day while I was unloading, I was having trouble getting the load out. It was stuck rice mill. Rice mill has a high moisture content and gets packed down from the movement of the trailers while being pulled down the road. The only way to get it out is to hit the side of the trailer with a big rubber mallet. I would swing it like a bat and hit the side of the trailer as hard as I could. Then, I would get a shovel and stand just around the top of the trailer and poke at it. It was a workout and often took some time to get it all out of the trailers. Well, this one day Jose was behind me. Of course he wanted me to get my load off so he could unload his, it was at the end of the day and we all wanted to finish up and get home. And here I was with eighty tons of stuck rice mill.

Jose got out of his truck and started hitting the side of the trailer real hard, much harder than I could. We chatted a bit, and I found out he was married and had children but that he and his wife had separated recently. We continued to beat on the trailer until it was empty. I moved forward and to my surprise the back trailer just poured out. It took a few hits of Jose's rubber mallet and then it just flowed out into the silo feeder. As Jose and I stood watching the trailer unload, he started talking about his marriage and how sad he was. I asked some questions but mostly he talked and I listened. Once all the feed was out of the back trailer I pulled the truck forward and he helped me sweep up around the feeder pit. I looked at him and saw my brother in distress. I said, "I will pray for you and your wife."

He looked at me with a bit of a surprise in his voice and said, "Thank you." I just smiled.

Not long after that day, I was walking down the middle of the lined up trucks waiting to get loaded. Jose walked up to me with a picture of him and his wife. He told me that they were seeing each other again and that they had started going to church. He was so happy; I do not think I had ever seen him smile before. We spoke for a little bit, I expressed how happy I was for him and I truly was. As I was walking towards my truck, there was a surreal feeling about me, like I was floating. I noticed all the drivers out of their trucks laughing, talking, no bickering, then there was Mulchor sitting in his truck reading a Bible and smiling. He was truly enjoying what he was reading and I smiled too.

Later that day, I pulled up behind Pete. We were both waiting to unload and Pete was next. It was a lovely evening. What I recall about the time was that the sky was so beautiful. I got out of my truck for some reason or another just in time to find Pete bent over picking what looked like a beautiful purple weed from between a pavement crack. He was so concerned for it. He really did not even notice me there as all his attention was on saving this purple flowered weed. Once he got it out from between the pavement crack, he hurried towards his truck mumbling something about getting it some water.

He turned the corner of his truck and a wave came over me, a wave of peace. And I heard, "my work is finished here." Funny how I have never questioned those thoughts. There was a small part of me that thought, "Ahhh?" The rest of me just felt at peace.

Not long after that I was injured on the job and did not return to the trucking company that I worked for. Our work was done there.

We often feel our lives have little or no meaning. In truth our lives are not our own. We are all connected in a most profound way. And that which holds us together in the center of us all is the Father of all creation. He touches each and every one of us reminding us of His presence and His Love. There is not one of us who will not at some point in this life feel this, and know it is true.

Blessed are they that have not seen, and yet have believed. John 20:29

There will be great joy in Heaven on your homecoming, and the joy will be yours. For the redeemed son of man is the guiltless Son of God, and to recognize him is your redemption.
A Course in Miracles
OrEd.TX.12-8, 9

The Book

In 1994, I was given a book.

I was given *A Course in Miracles* by my dear friend; she had found it at a book sale and said to me that as soon as she saw it she thought of me. I was grateful of course, however, it was a big book, and I am not much of a book reader. I opened the book and read the introduction, (how it came about), and from that moment, I rarely put it down for two years.

I was so excited and deeply touched by the instructions I received from this beautiful book. The words spoke to the truth that dwelled within me. They spoke to the child of God, the one I saw in my awakening of home; the words spoke to my true self, my higher self. I was so eager to awaken the truth within me that I would wake up at 4:00 am. And there in that quiet place would be the Bible, the book and me. Sitting at the kitchen table, coffee and notepad in hand, I was amazed and honored when I came to the realization that I was a student of the teaching of *A Course in Miracles*.

I have since read the book more times than I can remember. I have carried it with me, read it in the rain, and sitting in my car during lunch. The books says, "This is a course in miracles... please take notes. And then, "this is a required course. Only the time you take is voluntary."

What I gained from this book? "A Course in Miracles" is profound, personal, and deeply spiritual. The book guided me to healing by learning forgiveness. My eyes were open and I saw the spirit of Christ in everyone. I remembered who I was, and that is a child of God, a child of Love, created in Love's image. I learned how to set judgment aside if only for a holy instant (a moment). I learned that as I heal, the world is healed with me. For no man is an island. To let go of the past by finding that there is nothing to forgive. I looked inside and found that all I had ever wanted was already given to me. Not by myself but by the one in whom I am from, the Creator of all things. I received instruction for all my many questions; I already knew the answer. The answer is always love.

The truth in One, is surely shared by All.

What I can say is that I have learned so much... if I were to write it down, I would write many books on the subject myself.

The Kingdom of Heaven is within you and all about you... when you see it in your brother you have seen it for everyone.
What the Course says is very simple:
Nothing real can be threatened.
Nothing unreal exists.
Herein lies the peace of God.
Think of light, formless and without limit, as you pass by the thoughts of this world. And do not forget that they cannot hold you to the world unless you give them the power to do so.
A Course in Miracles
W-44, 10

Instructions for Life

I am not here to advise anyone. I cannot tell you how to find inner peace. I am no more or no less than you are. All of God's children are on equal ground, rather you choose to believe it or not! I cannot instruct you on what you should do or what you should not do. What I can say is, "All who seek will find." There is but one way and that way is through love. Only love! In truth, nothing else exists. I can also say, "Forgive, forgive yourself for all the things you thought you have done, and all the things you think others have done to you." It is time we all stop playing the victim and the victimizers and allow our true selves to emerge. Do not be afraid of who you are. You are of God, who loves you beyond measure. And your light shines brighter than the Sun itself.

There is but One
This One always has been, and always will be
This One who is the Creator of all things
You and I are an extension of Him
He loves us, just as He loves His Oneself

I would ask that you at least acknowledge that truly nothing is as it seems. If you could step out of yourself for a moment and look with the eyes of love, you would immediately realize that this life is but a wonderful experience, and an experience is all it is.

We are all a part of God who is the Creator of all things. I am not God and you are not God, yet we are the children of God. We came to be through Him by His will and created in His image and likeness, not separate from Him ever. Not one thing we say or do will ever change that. Not even our own belief that it is so.

Please be silent for a moment and think of these words.

I have a message for you. Jesus would like us to listen to Him sometimes. He knows it is difficult for us to stop our mind long enough. Yet He has things to tell us, when we pray we ask Him so many questions, so many concerns, we ask for help, for healing... We ask for answers! We are not waiting for the answer to come. We are not listening, He often sends someone else to give us the answer or one of God's creations, a bird, butterfly so many ways to reach us. Yet we do not see them or understand that it is Him answering. He would like it if we would simply stand still and do nothing, think nothing after we have asked a question. Just be still and wait for the answer. It will come.

Just listen! His voice is quiet, he speaks from within us.

Reaching the Broken

To reach my Children I would recreate the Hell they made and walk through it with them. And they would see me and not be afraid.

One of the most humbling experiences I have had would be the sharing of my scars.

As I mentioned earlier in this story, I was a local truck driver. And through a series of mishaps the State Workman's Compensation decided to retrain me.

During this time, I attended several rounds of physical therapy. I also volunteered to help with a local interfaith group. The group served breakfast at a few locations in the area in which I live.

We would go down to a local park every Tuesday and Thursday morning. We served breakfast to many of the homeless folks. And afterwards, we would go down to Ninth Street. Now, Ninth Street was an older part of town where a string of battered motels lined the street on both sides. They had built them along what was once the old highway 99. Back in their heyday, I have no doubt they were in high demand. Back then they had no problems filling the rooms with busy travelers. As the years went by, they moved the highway. The motels became a place where the very poor would stay. Not just the financially poor but poor of spirit. These new inhabitants were the drug addicts, the prostitutes, and the alcoholics. They were all one and the same. The prostitutes were drug addicts. The alcoholics were prostitutes and drug addicts. Some of the motels had small kitchenettes, which are perfect for the long-term stay.

When we arrived at one of the motels, most of the folks would come out and get breakfast. They had an opportunity to look through boxes of free clothing that we had brought. I would go around and knock on doors of nearby motels. Just to let them know we were there with breakfast and other things they may need.

This one time I recall knocking and waiting, I could hear someone inside. So, I knocked again thinking they did not hear the knock, as the knock was not very loud the first time. A woman answered the door and it was obvious to me that she and a gentleman friend were in the middle of fixing drugs; they had the look of heroin addicts. They were both sitting around a small table that was by a window and the morning light was shining through. The light was just enough for me to catch a glimpse of their drug paraphernalia.

So, the woman opened the door with a bewildered look on her face, she was squinting from the morning light in her eyes.

I said, "Hi, hope… I hope I am not bothering you, we have breakfast and we also brought some clothes."

She looked at me and asked, "Where and how much does it cost?"

I said, "It is free" and I pointed to where we were set up across the street. There was a large crowd around the van where the food was being served.

She looked and said, "No thank you."

I stated, "I can bring you breakfast if you'd like, it's real good."

She hesitated for a moment and said, "OK," nodding her head.

I said, "Ok, then how many, two?"

She nodded her head, "Yes" and shut the door.

I ran across the street and grabbed a couple of breakfasts that were in takeout containers. I also grabbed something for them to drink and plastic silverware too. I took it over and knocked on the door.

She answered, took the food and said, "Thank you."

As she was closing the door, I added, "You may want to come over. We have lots of clothes today."

I went back across the street and started helping the others to serve breakfast. I turned and this woman was standing there getting coffee. I went up and said something. I noticed she had fresh track marks on her arms. I looked her in the eye and said, "I know what it is like. I used to take drugs."

She looked at me with disbelief and said something on the terms of, "I do not believe you." I held my arms out and pointed to my healed track marks. I pointed to the scars on my arms. She looked at them for a moment as if she couldn't believe her eyes. She looked at me while shaking her head. She looked at my arms, then at my face and back again. Smiling I said, "God, took it from me. He asked me for my life and I gave it to Him. My life was changed right then. I have not touched drugs since." I looked around and noticed that a few other folks were looking at my arms, including the pastor who led our little group.

As we were packing up, I noticed the woman and the pastor off to the side, talking. I did not hear the content of their conversation; yet I had a good feeling. She saw hope in me; she saw hope for herself. I felt the pastor was speaking the words she needed to hear. While I was standing there with my arms stretched out showing this woman my scars, I saw her for who she was. She was a beautiful being of light, hiding in the shadows of who she thought she was. I saw the light of Christ, the hope for the world, within the eyes of a drug addicted prostitute.

Truly nothing is as it seems.

What Scars are for

Several years have passed since my awakening to this life I chose. I continue on its journey and although it is not my own, it remains exactly as I would have it be. I follow where it leads and oftentimes I do not know why until the opportunity presents itself. With all its seeming ups and downs and challenges, I know I remain just as God created me... perfect in His sight, forever in His love. Just as we all are. There is nothing that is outside of Him.

The scars we have both inside and out are no longer what they appear to be. They are gentle reminders of what we once thought of ourselves. And when we can look at them without the feelings of how they got there, that is when we are truly healed of them, and of the circumstances surrounding them. When we can look at them without feelings of attack, or guilt, without fear... it is then that we are indeed healed.

Through our scars we are healed.

The Holy Spirit can and will use our scars to help others along their way. We can seek out those to assist or we can simply let them find us as they journey along the path back to God. As I have mentioned, we never leave God, we only believe our selves lost, forsaken, abandoned, unloved. A Course in Miracles would say, "It is either love, or fear." It is often said, "Love or a cry for love." When we stop to think of this, we know it is true. And we are glad of it.

I had a thought that I was separate from you, that we had conflict and I was isolated and victimized. I thought we were in competition and that I wasn't good enough. I thought you didn't care for me, I thought you had forgotten me. And for a moment I was lost, running through the deepest darkness. All the flashing signs that read 'exit' were missing. I felt alone, isolated and confused. Then I thought what do I know, I know nothing. And I heard your voice, you answered me, "God" you said, "You know God." In an instant the thought I had vanished, and love filled the void I once thought there.

The Scars

I had now spent nearly eighteen years as an Information Technology Professional thanks to the injuries I had received during one of my truck driving jobs and I was retrained.

I had accepted a contracting job in Oakland working for a health care group. It was a very long drive, 86 miles one way to this place and I often wondered why I was sticking with it. The job paid well, yet I was spending a large portion of it on car gas and upkeep, not to mention my health due to lack of sleep. I was into the eighth month of commuting to this job, feeling drained and ready for the contract to finish.

I often went out to a nice quiet place behind some buildings and would sit in the sun. Across the street from where I sat was an Alcoholics and Narcotics Anonymous meeting place. I would often watch groups of those who wished to be free of their addictions come and go.

A small group of young people caught my attention. I had witnessed them leaving so many times, maybe because they were a bit loud; they would come out of the meeting happy and making joyous sounds. I felt happy for them, and saw them for who they were, shining children of God; they all looked to have a glow about them.

One time towards the very end of my contract, instead of leaving as they normally did, they walked across the street to where I was sitting. They were talking about the meeting amongst themselves and exchanging cigarettes. A few of them sat down just across from me. Two young men and a young woman, along with a few others stood at a distance. The young woman asked me if I had a light and as it happened, I did. I stood up, reached into my pocket and handed it to her. There was some light chitchat between us and I sat back down.

As I sat listening to their conversation about drug use, I began to feel moved, moved to say something. My opportunity came when one of the young men stated, "If you ask me, the way out of it is through God." He had a smile on his face and moved his arms and hands in a strong show of expression. All the others sitting and standing around nodded their heads in agreement. I spoke up and said, "That is what I did, I gave my life to God and He took it from me. I spent the eighties as an intravenous drug user."

The young man asked, "What did you take?"

I said, "Meth mostly, I tried heroin but I did not like throwing up and towards the end, the last year I took cocaine."

He said, "That is heavy stuff, that's hardcore." And he looked at me with a look of disbelief on his face, his head was downwards and his eyes were looking straight at me as if to say; "I do not believe you." The others there all had a look of disbelief as well. I could only imagine their impression of an intravenous drug user, the worst they had ever seen, and hoped they would never get that bad. Here I was with my business casual attire, slacks, and a blazer.

I had the appearance of someone who had walked the straight and narrow all their life. And yet I am telling them that I was a drug addict too.

I have heard it said that a picture tells a thousand words. I asked, "I can prove it to you, do you want to see the scars, I have track marks?" They all nodded their heads. I stood up and removed my blazer, pulled my sleeves up and walked over towards the young man and the woman that were sitting across from me. The young man stood up and met me halfway. I stretched both of my arms out, and as he began to exam them I pointed to each scar, some pronounced, others faded but visible. He was nodding his head yet still seemed not quite convinced and then I turned my left arm over and showed him the one I had on the back side. The young woman asked, "Are they tracks?"

The young man said, "They sure as hell look like it, yup...

they're tracks." As he nodded his head yes to the others that were standing nearby he motioned over for the young woman to come look too.

She said, "No I believe you." She looked at him and then at me in wonderment. The others that were sitting and standing walked over to take a look for themselves.

One young man took a quick lean in towards me, looked and said, "Yup they're real." And then he asked; "How?" We were in the middle of a very busy area. I can only imagine what passersby thought as they went about their day, seeing me standing in the center of a group of people with both my arms stretched out while they were being examined.

As I went to sit back down, I started telling the story, "I was stuck in a world I created apart from God, set apart from the whole; I had an abusive boyfriend that I couldn't get away from. I tried everything I could think of to get away from it and nothing worked. That is because I was looking in the places that could not help me. Until about 9:00 one night, sitting in a car in the middle of a driveway, I cried out to God and He answered me. I went through everything I had done to get away from the drugs and the boyfriend, naming each one aloud. I said, "Only you can take this from me." I was crying so hard it hurt and I could not hold my head up. I cried out, 'Lord this hurts.'

"I heard His voice asking, 'Trust me.'"

"I said, 'I want to, but I do not know how.'"

"I heard Him say, 'That is enough.' Then what felt like a ton of bricks was lifted off my chest, I felt something leave, the pain was gone and everything around me was lit up, illuminated. It was as if the air was brighter."

"I had stopped crying and asked, 'What do I do now?'"

"I heard His voice say, 'It is OK, you can go into the house, everything will be different in the morning.' The next morning the boyfriend that I could not get away from left and I have not seen him since. I have had no thoughts of taking drugs. God took it from me instantly. Not everyone will experience that, but God will take it from you if you allow it; if you give it to Him."

They were all listening to the story. I felt they knew God would help them. It was obvious He was working in their lives. I could see it! I went on to say, "My only advice is not to let the world bring you down. You have changed, you are not the same yet the world still sees you as you were."

The one young man who first looked at my arms asked, "What... the world?"

I said, "Yes all the ones you know, they will not recognize that you have changed. They will see you as the same; just do not let that get you down.

"They will eventually see that you have changed, that you are not the same but it will take time. Especially your family and close friends, give them time. What matters is that you know and that is all. Do not hold anything that you have done in the past against yourself, as you are no longer that person.

"Learn to forgive starting with you. If you feel the need to tell someone you are sorry, tell them, if they accept it, wonderful, if they do not, it does not matter. Then it is on them, you have done your part."

As they walked off, they each thanked me for sharing my story. I smiled, nodded my head and said, "Thank you."

I am and will continue to be grateful for the life God has given me. I could not help but feel that He will work in their lives as He has mine, for the reason that they are willing to let go of what they had made of themselves. And that they have chosen to live the lives that God has given them.

As I went back into work that afternoon, as I walked back across the street, I felt it was time; my work was done.

My contract came to an end not long after that faithful meeting. Nothing is by chance! For all things there is a time and a season under Heaven.

The world sees us as lacking and unworthy, Our Father sees us whole and wholly loving. For Love made me like itself.

We condemn/judge ourselves by the same measure we condemn/judge others. The reason being there is but One. We look for fault in our brothers by not seeing that the fault is within us. Why would we condemn ourselves when we can be happy instead?

Do not judge so that you will not be judged. For in the way you judge, you will be judged and by your standard of measure, it will be measured to you. Why do you look at the speck that is in your brother's eye, but do not notice the log that is in your own eye? Matthew 7:2

The Temple of Living Stones

For several years, I thought I was procrastinating on writing the Heaven story. Seems I would often talk myself out of it. Even the little ego played its part by having me think that after I wrote the story, I would die. One morning some years back, between waking and sleeping I had a thought. If you write the story, I will die and so will you. That is why you are here. As if this is my one and only role to play, in this thing we call life. How silly! The ego is a very loud chattering, fearful thing. I often find myself laughing at it. Then there are times I comfort it as if it were a child crying in the dark. And yes, more times than not I identify with it. There is much to say about the ego; however, we will leave that for someone else to explain. The one thing I can say is that it is everything that we are not. Yet it has convinced us that it is who we are. "Yup, I told you it was funny."

As I mentioned, there seemed to be much procrastination on my part. There were moments when I even felt guilty about it. Then I would hear, "For all things there is a season, a time and a place. Nothing is as it seems, and all is as it should be." In which I fully did not appreciate or understand for that matter, until I started a new job in November 2012.

It was yet another Information Technology job. This one was much closer to my home than the last job. I was grateful for the opportunity and relieved I did not need to commute five hours per day any longer. The job was a bit below my skills, yet I did not see it that way.

I had been working at this new job for only a short time when I met Hector. He seemed familiar to me. There was a glow about him, a very familiar glow. I had asked him, "Where have I seen you before? You look familiar." We went through a list of ideas, yet none of them panned out. We both came to the conclusion that it may have been in passing, like in a grocery store, the movies, something on those terms. After all, we had both been living in the same city for some time.

Together we had many a conversation on spirituality. We spoke of theology and religion. I told him I was a *Course in Miracles* student. I had started back in 1994, yet had just recently picked it up again. He was interested, and stated that his roommate had taught the Course some years back. He also mentioned that he had attended a group where they covered quotes from different spiritual leaders and he named a few. He did not seem completely satisfied with the spiritual information he had been receiving. I recognized him as a searcher, a seeker of the truth. How often have we looked outside of ourselves for that which we have, for that which dwells within us? How often have we been mistaken?

Within the core of All dwells the memory of home... We often become confused and think, it is in a person, a place or a thing, and when we find it is not... we continue. When we do find it, and be assured we will... there is nothing more... we could ever possibly want.

One afternoon Hector and I went to lunch. On the way he asked me, "So tell me about A Course in Miracles. What is your view of it?"

I said, "There is so much that can be said of the Course. Yet the Course summons it up in the Introduction."

Nothing real can be threatened. Nothing unreal exists. Herein lies the Peace of God.
A Course in Miracle Teache- Intro 2:1, 2, 3, 4

I went on to add, "To me it is learning to forget that which we think we know, so we can remember what we have known all along." He asked me about the lessons, and stated he was interesting in studying it. I let him know that I would send him some information on it. I said, "The Course is free. There are several websites now. I use both the book and the websites."

We had light chitchat during lunch. We spoke a bit more about the Course and some of the spiritual material he had studied. He stated that he had been practicing T'ai Chi Chi'ian for over 15 years. He enjoyed the depth that practicing this art had brought into his life.

It was on the way back from lunch that he said something that sparked my memory. He said, "I think we are all fragmented pieces of God. God got bored, because He knew all there was to know, and broke Himself up into trillions of pieces. And gradually all the pieces of God find their way home again, until finally God is put back together. He knows all there is to know again, then He breaks up and it starts all over. I think it is something like that."

I replied, "That is it." I did not elaborate, yet at that moment I knew where I had seen Hector before. He was the one in the front of Heaven. He was the one that waved his arms to get my attention. He was the one who knew me, yet I did not recognize him. He was the one who was the last light being to enter the spiritual mound, which became the altar of God.

In whom the whole structure, being joined together, grows into a holy temple in the Lord. And in him you too are being built together to become a dwelling in which God lives by his Spirit. Ephesians 2:21-22

The forming of the spiritual mound also reminds me of something I have read from the Gnostic Gospels. The gospels were hidden in the desert of Egypt for nearly two thousand years. Some of which are to be found in the Holy Bible, while some never made it that far. The Gospel of Thomas was one that did not find its way. Yet I deem it no less significant than the ones that did.

Jesus said:

I am the light that is over all. I am the All.
The All came forth out of me. And to me the All has come.

Split a piece of wood – I am there.

Lift the stone, and you will find me there. Gospel of Thomas 77

And then again Jesus said to them:

When you make the two into one, and when you make the inside like
the outside and the outside like the inside and the above like the
below – that is, to make the male and the female into a single one, so
that the male will not be male and the female will not be female – and
when you make eyes instead of an eye and a hand instead of a hand
and a foot instead of a foot, an image instead of an image, then you
will enter the kingdom. Gospel of Thomas 22

I thought of it for a few days, wondering if I should tell him of the Heaven experience and what I saw there. The Holy Spirit said, "Yes, tell him." From that moment on, I waited for a good time to tell him. The, Holy Spirit said, I would know when the time was right.

It just so happened one day not long after our lunch together, Hector and I were alone in a bit of a secluded area at our work.

I said, "Hector, I have something I need to tell you, but please do not be alarmed. I mean it is a good thing!" He had a look on his face as if to say, "OK, I am listening with caution." At this point he had no idea what I was about to say.

I said, "Some years ago, I had a dream, well at least at first I thought it was dream. Until one morning, I asked God if it were real or not. Later that afternoon, I was driving through Livermore looking for a radio station. I heard a man say, 'Remember that dream you had the other night about Heaven and you were wondering if it was real or not?'

"Well the man said, 'Stay tuned' and when he came back music was playing. He said, 'Remember that dream you had the other night about Heaven and you were wondering if it were real or not, well I am here to tell you it was real, you were there.' I went on to tell Hector more, about me calling the station a few days later and talking to the announcer. His name was Scott Osborn."

I told Hector, "Heaven was all golden and bright, yet it did not hurt my eyes because I am a spirit, I am a golden spirit and everyone is there, and so are you." I said, "I saw you there, you were in the front and you waved at me, I waved back but I did not recognize you. At first, all I saw was golden spirit, and as I focused, you seemed to take on an appearance. It even looked as though you were wearing clothes but it was more like an outline of clothes and I could see your face. The image is like that of a negative photo except you were this beautiful golden light and kind of cloud shaped."

I went on to say, "In the front there were other spirits that were making a mound; they were making a spiritual mound with their spirit bodies. You waved at me, and I waved back. I watched you look behind us and you had a look of such awe on your face. And then you turned, ran and leaped, dove right into the center of the spirit mound. I watched as you conformed until I could no longer distinguish where you were." Hector had a smile on his face, and I could tell that he believed me.

I went on to tell him that Jesus was there on a wide sparkling walkway that looked like clear diamonds or comets. It had movement like a river.

He said, "Jesus?" With a bit of dismay in his voice, I explained that to me, that is who He is. To you, He may be someone else, as in truth we are all one and the same. I told him, "We look just like

Him, exactly. We are all beautiful golden spirits of different shades of gold and yellow and within our center there is a round place that has what looks like stars, moving around in a clockwise pattern." I also stated that they were of different colors, some red, blue, yellow, green and lots of white, bright white.

I went on to say, "Jesus moved from around where I was standing to the front and He moved so fast. All I saw was a streak of light. He went to the top of the spirit bodies that now looked to be solid and flat on top. As I stood there watching Him, I noticed to my left something begin to flash. It was dome-shaped and clear yet bright. In the center, I noticed another figure; this one was faint and yellow. As the center figure became brighter, the large dome-shaped one became brighter and grew until that was all that was there. I saw three become one. To me, this One was God manifested. For what purpose, I do not know. As the Creator of all things is everywhere, there is no place God is not. This One had bright lights of many colors, which spun like a vortex in a clockwise manner. I found myself watching these lights in pure awe. As I watched, I noticed they looked like galaxies and universes."

I said, "Bolts of lightning extended from Him."

Hector asked, "Lightning?"

I said, "They were more like large beams of light, the color of lightning. I saw two beams, one to my left and one to my right. They went into the beings of light, the spirit bodies. I had a thought. 'Tell my children about God.'

"As I watched, I saw a very bright light. I said, 'No.' Then I woke up and I was back here." I then said, "Hector, this dream, this vision this awakening happened twenty years ago."

There was some talk between the two of us and then Hector sat down. He had a puzzled look on his face and said, "Was it twenty years ago or in the future?"

I said, "I know it does not make any sense does it?"

He said, "I mean we are alive, how can it be?"

I said, "I think it is happening right now, we just cannot see it." The man on the radio said, 'God wants you to know you are still there.'

I said, "Which makes me think I never left, and if I never left neither have you. None of us have, heaven is our home. I think we are sleeping or I am sleeping; it is confusing, but I trust it is true, even though I do not understand it. Heaven is right here, we simply cannot see it because we have our eyes closed. We are blind to it. Just because we cannot see it does not mean it is not here. Our perception of time is just that, perception. We are timeless, residing in the only place that exists, perceiving of time; we are dreaming of that which is not."

It was wonderful for me to share the vision with Hector. I asked him if I could add this chapter to the story. He said, "Yes."

I asked, "So what is your middle name?"

He said, "Why?"

I said, "Well you do not want me to use your real name do you?"

Hector said, "Go ahead I do not mind, it is OK."

I am grateful to my brother Hector for allowing this part of the story to be shared.

I realized after this that all things have their place. Although I felt I was procrastinating all these years, I can now see that I was simply waiting to meet the one that waved.

I received an email from Hector just a few days ago and this is what he had to share.

I was studying Masonic lore and came across this:
The Temple made of wood and stone must crumble and decay, but there's an unseen fabric, which shall never pass away; Age after age the Masons strive to consummate the plan, But still the work's unfinished which our forebears began; None but immortal eyes may view, complete in all its parts, The Temple formed of living stones —
the structure made of hearts.

It made me think of your dream/vision of the altar. It makes me wonder if it wasn't foreshadowing something.
hh

As I sit here now contemplating what is real and what is unreal, I realize that I do not know what anything is for. I trust, however, that we move in each other. Our lives are not our own, they are intricately shared, entwined in and with one another. Together we live and move within the Spirit of Creation. We are joined in perfect Peace and Love beyond anything we can possibly imagine. We are in the Father, the Creator, the Source of Life, the Beginning and End, the Great I AM... I AM what I AM. The name makes no difference. Call this One what you will as it will never change who He is. There is nothing that we can do or say that can or will ever change that. Despite what we have been told, trust that we are safe and sound, loved and cherished. We are not what we think we are. We are what God has created us to be. We will remain just as God created us, beautiful golden beings of light reflecting both inward and outward the Father's love and light.

What is our perception of God? We would consider our perception multiplied by an amount so great that it cannot be counted. It is here we live and here we dwell; it is here we have peace.

The Continued Path

The life that I have chosen has continued on the path back to the place I have never left; back home to the Heaven memory. Not just my home, but Our Home.

I attend a Unity Church now, where I am at home with my spirituality. It is a place where the truth in me is reflected and made manifest, a place where sin is error and love is all; where positive thinking brings positive results; where to seek God means to look within. I am happy!

All of this is a part of my beautiful story, the memories, the hard times, all the many mistakes and the friends I have met along the way. This is my role at least for this time, for this moment.

The book, *A Course in Miracles*, played its part too. Although I put it down for many years, I would often open the book and read a lesson or a passage. One of my favorites, which I feel sums the book up is, "The Forgotten Song."

The Forgotten Song

The blind hate the world they made.
They hate the world they learned through pain.

Everything they think is in it serves to remind them that they are incomplete and bitterly deprived.

Thus they define their life and where they live, adjusting to it as they think they must, afraid to lose the little that they have.

And so it is with all those who see the body as all they have and all their brothers have.

And so they adjust to loneliness, believing that to keep the body is to save what little they have.

Listen, and try to think if you remember of what we speak of now.

Listen… Perhaps you catch a hint of an ancient state not quite forgotten; dim, perhaps, and yet not altogether unfamiliar, like a song whose name is long forgotten, and the circumstances in which you heard completely unremembered.

Not the whole song has stayed with you, but just a little wisp of melody, attached not to a person or a place or anything particular. But you remember, from just this little part, how lovely the song, how wonderful the setting where you heard it; and OH how you loved those who were there and listened with you.

The notes are nothing.

Yet you have kept them with you, not for themselves, but as a soft reminder of what would make you weep if you remembered how dear it was to you.

You could remember, yet you're afraid, believing you would lose the world you learned since then. And yet you know that nothing in the world you learned is half as dear as this.

Listen… and see if you remember an ancient song you knew… so long ago and held more dear than any melody you've taught yourself to cherish since.

Beyond the Body, beyond the Sun and Stars,

Past everything you see and yet somehow familiar, is an arc of golden light that stretches as you look into a great and shining circle.

The circle fills with LIGHT before your eyes.

The edges of the circle disappear, and what is in it is no longer contained at all.

The LIGHT expands and covers everything, extending to infinity forever shining with no break or limit, anywhere.

Within it everything is joined in perfect continuity.

It is impossible to imagine that anything could be outside, for there is nowhere this LIGHT is not!

This is the vision of the SON of GOD, whom you know well.

Here is the sight of him who knows his FATHER.

Here is the memory of what YOU are, a part of this, with all of it within, and joined to all surely as all are joined in you.

Accept this vision that can show you this, and not the body.

You know the ancient song, and you know it well.

Nothing will ever be as dear to you as this ancient hymn of LOVE the SON of GOD sings to his father still.

And now the blind can see, for that same song they sing in honor of their Creator gives praise to them as well.

The blindness that they made will not withstand the memory of this song.

They will look upon the vision of the SON of GOD, remembering who he is they sing of.

What is a miracle but this remembering?

And who is there in whom this memory lies not?

The LIGHT in one awakens it in ALL.

When you see it in your brother you are remembering for EVERYONE.

From a Course in Miracles

T-21, 4:10

The eyes of man are blind. The meaning of this is that we have chosen to see that which is not there. And blind to that which is right before us.

The Voice for God

Although there is no past, there are memories or so it seems. I can look back upon them with gladness and with gratitude. Truly, for all things there is a reason. I am a willing participant in this life.

I have had many a conversation with that voice that spoke to me in the closet and in my car. I still call Him Lord, although He is not above us. This He has made clear.

I once asked Him about my experience in Heaven, my memory or what seems like a memory. He explained to me that although it seems like something I have experienced in the past, it is happening now. And that not one moment has passed in Heaven since my return to the place where I think I am.

I think I am in a world, I think I am in a body. He explained that all I think I am and all I think of those around me both near and far, everything I see is not what it appears to be. Nothing is as it seems.

I asked Him about Jesus, to me, the one I saw was Jesus, even though His appearance is not like that of any pictures I have ever seen of Him. And no one said to me, "This is Jesus" or, "I am Jesus." There was none of that. There was a simple knowing. What I can say is that I know Him and He knows me. He knows me very well and He is happy to see me. If I were to find an image as to what this one looked like or resembled, it would come very close to the three dimensional image on the Shroud of Turin.

His answer to my question, "I am what you perceive me to be, I am you and you are me, we are one in God. I am neither higher nor lower; I am all."

I asked Him about those who awaken and do not belong to a religious faith or have no spiritual background. Who will be there for them, what of other faiths? My teacher said, "They are all one and the same."

This was my answer. He also assured me that all would awaken. He said, "It is impossible that anyone or anything be left behind. My love, how can anyone or anything be misplaced or lost if it never left in the first place? There is no other place to go."

I asked Him a similar question, "Why Ezekiel, why John, why me and so many others?"

I was given the same answer, "You are one and the same."

I thought about that for some time. Then I asked a question that would open the possibility of reincarnation. I was seeing this answer as a possibility that the spirit I am could possibly be the Biblical Ezekiel, and that of John of the New Testament. Had I many lives with one similar role to show a vision of Heaven, a vision of home to share with those who slumber?

My answer, "We are all here now." I thank you Father for answering me in such a way that I can understand.

I asked Him about the man in the laundromat. "Why did he call me John?"

He said, "Did he get your attention?"

I said, "Yes, and it was so profound that it stayed with me."

Holy Spirit said, "do you recall the man saying, 'Open your eyes child, and don't be afraid?'"

I said, "Yes... I did not understand him, I told him I was awake."

Holy Spirit said, "Your brother was a willing participant, he was listening. It was me who spoke through Him to reach you."

I asked, "Who are the angels that were there waiting for me? I think they were the same ones who spoke to me while I was awake in Heaven."

My answer, "Yes they were the same. Did you notice when you turned to look behind you how you could not see them even though they were speaking to you?"

I said, "Yes."

Holy Spirit said, "That is because they are an aspect of you. A part of your own mind, they are beings because they are extensions of you. They are your creations. Just like the little part of you that stayed in the church. All of God's children have many aspects of their own selves. Most of which appear to be created in time, but not of it. That is because they are created from love, yet they have always been just as you have always been. For that reason, they are a part of you. You were created by thought and through love, you are not of time. You are timeless just as your Father is timeless. And your creations are created in the image and likeness of you who is love."

Holy Spirit: "Do you recall the parable when I spoke of the children saying:

For I say to you, that their angels in heaven continually see the face of My Father who is in heaven. For the Son of Man has come to save that which was lost. (Matthew 18: 10, 11)

"My love, I used the children as an example. I was not just speaking of the children who were playing nearby. I was referring to All God's children. Your true self continually sees the face of the Father, as you stand before Him even now. You are an observer of the thoughts you are thinking now. That is why you cannot be harmed or changed or made into that which you are not."

Holy Spirit: "There is a place within the golden spirit bodies that so amazed you that when you saw them you wondered what it was that you were seeing."

Me: "Yes, I did not know what the circles of spinning lights were. Those lights like comets, like shooting stars that spun within the center of all the spirit bodies. That was the Water of Life, right?"

Holy Spirit: "Yes, you are correct. The living water that you saw are creations; Beings, created through love. Unique, just as you are unique yet one with all. Your creations dwell within you just as you dwell within the Father. Your creations are extensions of the Creator of all things just as you are the extension of the Creator of all things. Your creations love and adore you. They know you, because they came through you from the Father. They are your children, created through love. They are as much a part of you as they are a part of me."

We are like a precious diamond with many facets... each reflecting both inward and outward... the light and love... of God.

We all live in a state of miracles. Nothing has ever happened to us without our permission. In this place, life on earth, I dreamt I shattered into eight billion pieces. As love would have its way, step by step, all the broken, lonely pieces of my, oneself... reunite. Returning to the place they have never left. They all come back to their source through the miracle of forgiveness. Through Forgiveness of that which never was, releasing all we thought we had done.

Curtain Call

It is said, all expressions of love are maximal. I believe this is true. If anything is not born from love, then it is a call for love.

This story would suggest love is something much more than what we can see. It is more than we can feel with our hands. Love is so much more than all this. We can see actions of love, but we cannot see love itself, not with our eyes.

We can feel it within us stirring, warming us, overpowering all of our senses or so it seems. It grows until love is all we know, and that is Love itself, love created us to be itself. Love has no beginning and no end.

I envision a very large dam filled to the top. Then I see all the floodgates fully open all at the same moment; water gushes forward, arched out with a force that clears the river beneath it of all debris. The river runs strong, swift, and pure, flowing forward sustaining life everywhere it goes. The river is life to all it passes. That is the truth of love's gift within us. It gushes forth from our eternal source who is God, who is our Father and Creator of all things. And it clears all the debris we created to block the flow of love. Love flows from within us, without a word, without a touch, yet this flow is strong, swift, and true. It is not what the world would think love is; no it is what Love would have us feel. There can be nothing else, as only love exists. We are Spiritual Beings also known as Angels of Light, the Children of God. We are pretending to be human. We are masquerading as individuals that are separate from one another, in both body and thought. What a great idea that we have this hide-and-seek that we play. How else would we have experienced that which we do not know?

There will come a moment when each of us will realize that Love is all there is. And in that moment everything that is not of love will fade away and be no more.

As this story comes to a close, we cannot help but think of all the Goobers in our lives. The ones that taught us the toughest lessons, the hardest lessons; the ones that showed us what it felt like to hate and be hated. We found them in the darkest corners of our minds, hiding and waiting to pounce. We stood at the gallows and cheered as we imagined the noose placed around their necks. We sighed with relief as we watched them take their last breath. It was then that we became the instruments of our own demise. What we had not realized is what we were doing to ourselves by seeing this darkness and the hate that we felt. That it would lead us to recognize the light. It is recognizing the darkness that enables us to recognize the light that was there all along. We hide the light from ourselves, thus enabling us to experience that which we have not known. And that which we have not known are all expressions of fear.

What if, beyond a doubt, you knew that if you judged another person you were equally judging yourself? And what if, beyond a doubt, you knew that if you forgave another person that you would truly be forgiving yourself? What if, you knew beyond a doubt, that as you loved another person, you truly love yourself? What if, everything you have taught yourself to believe is wrong? What if by judging yourself, you have judged the whole world? And by forgiving yourself you have set the world free!

And what if, by loving everything you are, that everyone in the world would love themselves as well? And in that holy instant the world and all that is in it will be changed. Heaven and Earth will be as one. I am asking, What if?

The second coming is not as the world has envisioned. That thought was brought about by fear and dread. The second coming is now. It is as God would have it be.

When you see the spirit of Christ in your brother you have seen it for everyone.

Imagine if you will, a large stadium filled with everyone you have ever met. All of them, everyone from the perceived time you came into this world until this very moment. There are those you have yet to meet, or so you think. Yes they are all here as well.

In this stadium there is a very large stage with curtains that seem to reach beyond walls. As you were entering the stadium you noticed a bright white outline of light surrounding the trees and the buildings. You noticed this light surrounding your arm as you reached out to open the door. And as you enter the stadium you are amazed at how many people are here. Everyone in this place has a familiar face and a glow about them. They too are surrounded by that bright white light. It surround everything and everyone.

The feeling is jubilant, there is no place we would rather be than right here. As you make your way through the crowd there are hugs and handshakes, and a little girl hands you flowers. There is a man just in front of you smiling with that familiar glow. He is motioning for you to follow him.

He leads you to the front of the stage, and a symphony orchestra is waiting for you. You are handed a baton. You say to the one that handed it to you, "I do not know how to lead an orchestra."

The one who handed you the baton leans in and whispers in your ear, "Oh but you do. You are the conductor and composer of this life you chose. Only you know the music that will play. You know the scenes, the life events the hard times, the laughter and the joy. You know it because you created it. It is your masterpiece."

You take your place and tap the baton on the conductor's podium twice. The orchestra begins a soft melody as the curtain starts to rise. The play begins with the moment that you were conceived. Some moments of your life seem to fly by with the music sounding like a fast galloping horse. Other moments are slow and gentle like that of a soft flowing spring. And oh yes! There is suspense as it plays out before your eyes. There are mass moments of clarity and confusion. You cannot count the many times you were both victim and hero. How often you fall and how often you pick yourself up, brush yourself off and move on. There were a few times when you fell and just laid there crying for help. There was always that one that rushed to your aid. Someone helped you stand up and brushed you off, wiped your tears and helped you to laugh again. Reminding you that nothing is as bad as it often seems.

Then there are the horrific scenes where darkness steps in and plays its part. These are the moments you seemed lost. Fear filled your mind, and all plummeted. Hope was gone. This is your darkest hour of grief, where guilt and unforgiveness have its way. This is where you are broken.

In this place of your darkest hour comes a messenger, maybe a person, a hummingbird, a twinkling star, or a song on the radio. This messenger has many forms yet it will always appear in the darkest of moments. This is where you find that darkness has no power over you. It is here you realize that truth at last. You see that the darkness you created can be undone. Not by fighting it or hating it, but by love. At this moment, love comes gushing forth from deep within. You remember that you are none of these things, but that you are love created in its image. And light returns to your mind. Now where there was once doubt there is trust, with you knowing beyond a doubt, that all is well!

The play comes to an end. The curtains close. The one who handed you the baton reaches out his hand and you give it back to him. You, the composer, are called to the stage. As you walk up the stairs, you look out into the stadium. All you can see is a very bright light that covers everything. You stand stage left looking towards center stage. The curtain begins to rise and out from behind it come a vast company of players. Each of them smiling, there is that glow about them. It is much brighter now than it was at the beginning. The audience clap. The players bow and make their way upstage. They take their places on stairs that fill a good part of the stage. Then, from both the left and the right stage are those who came and went in your life. The sidekicks, the mentors and let us not forget, the skeptics. They bow and take their place on the stairs of both left and right stage. And finally, here they come, the main players. The audience clap and cheer although you cannot see them through the bright light. You can hear them and you know they are there. The main players bow and bow again towards you. Your heart is full of gratitude. Some of the main players show a character trait, a certain look, a stance and you cannot help but laugh.

Beaming outwards from the side wings off stage shines a beautiful light that illuminates everything with a golden hue. You stand in amazement. This light is so beautiful, words cannot express the feeling you have while seeing it.

Then out to center stage walks the villains, the "Goobers" of your life. The audience roar! You are filled with so much love and compassion it cannot be contained. You are laughing so hard that you begin to cry. They are not the dark characters whom they portrayed. They are the brightest of all. Their eyes sparkle like spinning lights. You remember how much you love them.

You are so elated by this memory of love that you are finding it difficult to stand. Two of the villain characters walk over to you and taking you by both arms, help you to stand. Ever so gently, they lead you to center stage. Here at center stage you are greeted by the "Goobers" of your life. For each one of them there is an embrace and you express your gratitude by saying a very heartfelt "thank you." One reaches out and wipes a tear from your cheek, smiling as he does so. As he reached out his arm, you noticed you could vaguely make it out; there is so much golden light. You have forgiven all you thought you had done and all you thought that was done to you. Together, the villains and you hold hands. You all walk out to the edge of the stage and take the final bow. As you raise your head all that are there with you are bright golden beings of light. The dream of separation is over... the atonement is complete. We are home; we are One with one another. We are One with God, whom we have never left, nor from whom we have ever been separate.

Brother, forgive me now. I come to you to take you home with me.
And as we go, the world goes with us on our way to God.
A Course in Miracles

There is a light, like a flame in you that cannot be extinguished. As you are that light you are that flame. Our true selves are created in the likeness and image of the Father, from whom we are of. We are an intricate part of the Creator of all things and with one another. We are now and always have been. As the Father Is, so are we... Never to be born, never to perish, but to continue on for we and the Father are one.
And so it is!

Love is all that exists... there is no place it is not.

To everyone who has ever judged me... Thank You!
To those who have caused me pain... Thank You!
To those who hate me... Thank You!
To those who have helped me heal... Thank You!
To those who Love me... Thank You!

I thank the darkness, I thank the shadows.
I thank the light, that illuminates all things.
I thank you for being here with me now.

Thank you, thank you!

I love you, I appreciate you and I behold the Christ in you.

You are a Spiritual Being pretending to be human. You have chosen this life.
Now, go play!

Shared Thoughts

Mine Enemy

Have you ever heard the phrase, "I am my worst enemy?"

This, I would I keep in mind as I set out to define exactly who mine enemy is. With the thought in mind once defined, I would do as I have been instructed, as we have all been instructed. Pray for your enemy.

I know that the things I hold against others, I likewise hold against myself. I know that if I forgive, I shall be forgiven. As I "forgive, take my sins away." These come from the one prayer Jesus gave us, the Lord's Prayer, or Our Father.

Some years ago, as I moved through a spiritual evaluation (and will continue moving for that matter), I found it necessary to heal from past hurts; traumas that I felt were holding me down. This is something that we all must do if we're ever truly to be free. The past is similar to a cement block tied around our necks. We will never soar, as we rightfully should, as long as this past remains.

I am reminded of a game we neighborhood kids used to play: "The Moshmontes and the Dukisoas."These were names created from yet another game, a rhyming game. For some reason those two names just stuck with us. The Moshmontes were the good guys. The Dukisoas, well imagine something unpleasant stuck to the bottom of your shoe. For example, dog-do, cat-do... need I say more? The Dukisoas were the bad guys. Now, of course nobody was really bad. We were all good friends that enjoyed playing with one another. That was an unspoken truth we all knew!

The Moshmontes and Dukisoas was a hide-n-seek game with a twist! We kids would often come together on a warm Saturday afternoon, ready for action. Our favorite choice was to play "The Game." We would divide into two groups. Which group would be the Moshmontes or the Dukisoas was left to fate with the toss of a coin.

After that, we would earnestly set about to play. We played our group's role in the game. The one and only defense the Moshmontes, aka the good guys, could employ was to hide. The Dukisoas, though they were bad guys, had all the power, or so it seemed!

The rules of our game were: we could hide in the yards of those children who participated in that session of the game; we could not either hide or seek in a kid's yard that wasn't playing. So, we knew our territories. We stayed within our own collective and various yards. That included front yards, backyards, sheds, bushes even rooftops, if you so dared. All outside places were permissible. We could not hide inside of our houses. Our parents didn't seem to care much for that!

When one of the Moshmontes (the good guys) was found, he or she would fall under the ever-changing rules of the Dukisoas. Once found, the Moshmontes would be corralled into one place. They were then carefully guarded by one or two Dukisoas. Finally, the inevitable came and all the Moshmontes were found, then the game would be over.

Our game would continue, sometimes, well into dark. We were exhausted, yet happy. Not only happy that we got to play the game but happy because we got to play with one another. It did not really matter which side one was on.

Some of you may wonder what I'm getting at, what's the point here?

It's not really a point; it's more of what if!

What if, in a place time dare not enter, we all stood together being our true selves with a mutual love, compassion, and respect for one another? And what if we agreed to play the game and accept whatever role fate offered us? And what if one of the rules was that we would temporarily forget our mutual love?

Yet all agreeing that a love so true could never be completely forgotten. And in a wisp of a moment, we would remember how much we loved one another. We would simply be happy that we got to play the game.

It has been said so many times, "Nothing is as it seems and all is as it should be."

August 12, 2000
Inspired by: *A Course in Miracles*

Nothing is Hidden

Darkness is from Fear.
Anything that is of fear is a nonexistent shadow,
Yet we believe there is darkness from fearful thoughts
Which we often try to hide.
Since nothing is hidden
Our goal would be to first accept nothing is hidden
And not try to hide it.
No judgment,
Only forgiveness.
This comes from that which exists
Only that which exists is LOVE...

The Key

We as humans in hope strive to get to a better place.
What we do not realize
Is that we are already there.
We have simply hidden it from ourselves,
It is God's will that we open our eyes
Even if for an instant;
And know that we are home
The key to awaken is within us
And that key is Love...

Everything is Temporary

Nothing comes to an end,
How can it if it never existed,
Only that which is of God exists
And that which is of God will never end.
Never die, never feel pain, or want for anything
We, Me, You are of God

Everything else is temporary
For our learning purpose, our remembering purpose.
We are playing in a make-believe place made up of make-believe ideas
That we made up.
A part of me wants to say we did it for fun
Yet we did it to grow through experience of that which we know not,
That which we did not know is the belief that we are separate from God and one another.
You have chosen this life
Enjoy!

Morning Thought

Rise and Shine
The world awaits your Light,
And with each moment
We allow love to flow from within us.
The world and all that is in it Rejoices
And is, exceedingly glad.

Love is Connection

Love is remembering who we are.
When we experience Love
We know who we are again.
And that feeling is what connects us all to one another.
I am in Love with all of you,
We are connected
We are One.

Bring Us to Believe

In this world we perceive ourselves in, we have allowed deception, for what reason we can't be sure.

Believing, that we have no control over the circumstances in which we place ourselves.

Often we allow ourselves to believe that we have faults, that we are unworthy, unlucky, unforgiving, we think us smart, we think us dumb, we think we are a body, not just a body but an unperfected body, one that needs changing.

We hide from ourselves the truth of which we are.

For what we are lives inside the body we think we have!

I put on this body; it is a mere shadow of that which is the grand illusion!

That brings us to believe that we are separate from one another and our Creator.

That brings us to believe that we can be hurt, deceived ,make wrong or right decisions.

I am not a name, I am not a body, I am not my relationships, I am not my job or my chosen profession, I am not the car I drive or the clothes I wear.

I need not food, nor money; I need no possessions at all.

I am not the thoughts I think; I am but an observer of thoughts.

I was never born, nor did I come to be and I will not die.

I know not past, nor future.

I have never felt pain of any kind.

Who am I?

I am one spirit, whole and holy.

I am you and you are I.

I am of the only place that truly exits.

In this Place Love is so pure and true that it has form, and that form is who we are.

No, we are not the fallen; I am growing by experiencing.

What I will be has yet to be seen, we only know that it will be
   WONDERFUL.
What we are no eyes have been, no words can describe, no
   thought can imagine.
I AM ONE SPIRIT WHOLE and HOLY, ONE ARE WE.
Nothing is as it seems, and all is as it should be.

October 19, 1999

All that is of Love

The Creator of all things is Love itself,
We being created in the image of Love
Are Love as well.
All that is of Love
Is bound eternally to Love who is God.
All that is not of Love does not exist
As Love cannot be anything else but Love...

Love Is

Love is everywhere we are
Love is in the air
The flowers,
The trees,
The grass,
The mountains,
The animals,
The crawling, climbing, swimming and slithering of creation.
Love is the ground in which we stand
Love is in everything and everyone we see,
There is no place I AM not.

The Core of All

Within the core of All dwells the memory of home.
We often become confused and think
It is in a person,
A place or a thing.
And when we find it's not...
We continue...
When we do find it,
And be assured we will
There is nothing more
We could ever possibly want.

A Great Calm

They say in the center of a Hurricane there is a great calm
When we stand in our place of peace
And calm
We are not affected by the storm of chaos all around.
We are but observing the darkened clouds,
Yet we stand in the Light of the Son.
No fears,
No worries,
All is passing,
Peace remembered
God's Love extending from us
Until the storms are no more.
"My child do you not know nothing can harm you?"

No Stone left Unturned

Not one stone left unturned, will forgiveness leave, as it is
     through forgiveness the world is saved.
You are called to choose.

Through our forgiveness, the world is saved.

True forgiveness finds nothing to forgive.

There is nothing so dear to us than the memory of who we are.

Messenger of God, each moment spent in silent listening is a moment; 100 brothers will hear God's voice.

The truth in one is shared by all.

Your innocence lights the way for others.

The light of love shines, as steadily and as surely as quietness that never can be disturbed…

Light beings are miracle workers. All are light.

You are a mirror of truth in which God shines His perfect light.

Focus on the good in others, and it will grow in you until good is all that you see, as you are good. You simply think you are not.

The truth in us is our innocence as pure as light.

Our innocence lights the way for others to see their innocence… One instant we spend in communion with Love… and a thousand hearts open to Love's truth… and a new world begins.

True forgiveness is forgiving one's self and…

The end of guilt!

Gratitude

Once again, it's time to sit and contemplate, for that which I am grateful. And as I have sat this morning watching the darkened sky turn light, I can't think of anything that I am not grateful for!

I would first be grateful for this realization. Would we start from the Joyful time we chose this life?

I would say thank you, to all my teachers and guides, who are both here and on the other side of the ever-thinning veil.

Yet the mirror words, thank you, would only be a drop in the vast sea of my true gratitude.

Maybe I could begin by thanking the darkness that once enveloped me, so that I could better recognize the light. The light of home that dwells in all people! Or would I choose those life experiences that enabled me to hold wide open the door so that others may enter. And for this the reward of remembering the place in which we are of and how it is we got here. So, I'll always know the way home.

I would naturally thank those who loved me, but what of those who loved me enough to play the role of my enemy? Just so that I could know what true forgiveness means by learning that true forgiveness only comes when we see that there is nothing to forgive!

Everything that we are and all that we've needed has already been given us.

Life here in this world is an experience to be cherished. Life that is full of joys, sorrows, beauty and pain, tears and laughter.

Maybe these words are better expressed in the book of Ecclesiastes:

To everything, there is a season and a time for every purpose under Heaven.

A time to be born, a time to die,
A time to plant, a time to reap,
A time to kill, a time to heal,
A time to laugh, a time to weep,
A time to build up, a time to break down.
A time to dance, a time to mourn,
A time to cast away stones, a time to gather stones together.
A time of love, a time of hate,
A time of war, a time of peace,
A time to embrace, a time to refrain from embracing,
A time to gain, a time to lose,

A time to rend, a time to sew,

A time for peace

To everything, there is a season, and a time for every purpose under Heaven.

There is nothing for which I am not grateful and for this, I am grateful!

3-24-2002

Death a Word

Death a word, just a word... to us as humans it means FEAR, the end of life.

We have elected to be in TIME. We do not belong to time!

As our place is in ETERNITY where our creator has placed us forever and ever and ever, on and on and on we never end!

Prepare you now for the undoing that never was.

Physical birth is not a beginning; it is a continuing.

Everything that continues was never born; all that continues is of the beginning as God is of the beginning.

All that exists is GOD who is LIGHT and LOVE, only this is real.

Remember always that you are LIGHT and LOVE.

In truth, there is no beginning and there is no end. That which is the beginning is the end and that which is the end is the beginning.

As I share with you, I have shared with myself.

As truth in one is shared by all, one are we.

We are not now or ever been separated from one another.

My Peace I give to you, as where I am, I would have you be

also.

10/29/1999

Trust

Do not be Afraid...Trust
It takes but a little willingness to let go of control
Of that which we have no control of...
And by doing so fear flees out thoughts
Knowing it was never ours...

The Miracle

The miracle is not our ability to Love...
The miracle is our ability to forgive ourselves
For all those things, we think we have done...
Moreover, to extend that forgiveness we have received to all...

Thank you for noticing
An Appointed Moment

We do not recall choosing this life, yet that is exactly what we did.

We chose to forget who we are, children of God His self, Beautiful Beings of golden Light.

We did this in order to experience all the emotions in their most profound sense.

We stepped into our roles knowing we would forget the great love we have for one another.

We left little hints for ourselves here and there.

Therefore, we would eventually remember how much we love one another, so we could remember that we are not separate from our Father.

In an appointed moment the veil we created will be lifted, and we the children of God will simply be happy; we got to play the game.

Ever Extending

Trust... In a holy instant we will be changed
In that place we will see how it is...
We can be as Christ...
We will see how it is...
We are One...
Our true selves are beyond all boundaries...
Never separate from God...
Brilliant lights, ever extending, our Father's Love...

Separation is but an Illusion

Just because one's eyes are closed doesn't mean he is blind.

Truth is given to all equally.

As the truth in One is always shared by all.

This truth is not given to some now and others later.

Everything we have ever needed or wanted is within us ALL now.

Our role is not to judge the self who believes I am fragmented and thinks myself separate.

Separation is but an illusion and a belief system in levels that do not exist.

Resources

A Course in Miracles, Author Jesus, (1972) original edition. Scribed by Helen Schucman, co-scribe Bill Thetford.

A Course in Miracles, Author Jesus, (1975) second edition. Publisher: (Foundation for Inner Peace). Scribed by Helen Schucman, co-scribe Bill Thetford, with Kenneth Wapnick.

All quotations from *A Course in Miracles* have been used with written permission from the publisher and copyright holder, second edition, (C) Foundation for Inner Peace, P.O. Box 598, Mill Valley, CA 94942-0598, www.acim.org and info@acim.org.

Biblical quotes, researched over the period of 6-1-13, 1-26-15, from http://biblehub.com/

Gospel of Thomas quotes, retrieved over the period 6-1-13, 1-26-15, from the Gnostic Society Library, The Nag Hammadi Library website location: http://www.gnosis.org/naghamm /got.html

Michael W. Smith song "Place in this world" from the album "Go West Young Man." released October 1, 1990

KYCC "Your Christian Companion" radio station, Stockton, California

Circle Books

Circle is a symbol of infinity and unity. It's part of a growing list of imprints, including o-books.net and zero-books.net.

Circle Books aims to publish books in Christian spirituality that are fresh, accessible, and stimulating.

Our books are available in all good English language bookstores worldwide. If you can't find the book on the shelves, then ask your bookstore to order it for you, quoting the ISBN and title. Or, you can order online—all major online retail sites carry our titles.

To see our list of titles, please view www.Circle-Books.com, growing by 80 titles per year.

Authors can learn more about our proposal process by going to our website and clicking on Your Company > Submissions.

We define Christian spirituality as the relationship between the self and its sense of the transcendent or sacred, which issues in literary and artistic expression, community, social activism, and practices. A wide range of disciplines within the field of religious studies can be called upon, including history, narrative studies, philosophy, theology, sociology, and psychology. Interfaith in approach, Circle Books fosters creative dialogue with non-Christian traditions.

And tune into MySpiritRadio.com for our book review radio show, hosted by June-Elleni Laine, where you can listen to authors discussing their books.